Photograph of the Author in 1916.

"LANGEMARCK"
AND
"CAMBRAI"

A WAR NARRATIVE

1914—1918

BY

CAPTAIN GEOFFREY DUGDALE, M.C.

The Naval & Military Press Ltd

❖

Reproduced by kind permission of the Central Library,
Royal Military Academy, Sandhurst

Published by
The Naval & Military Press Ltd
Unit 10, Ridgewood Industrial Park,

Uckfield, East Sussex,

TN22 5QE England

Tel: +44 (0) 1825 749494

Fax: +44 (0) 1825 765701

www.naval-military-press.com

© The Naval & Military Press Ltd 2005

TO

JACK WHITTINGHAM

(late Pte. 6th K.S.L.I.)

AUTHOR'S PREFACE.

This book contains a narrative of my personal experiences in the Great War. It is not intended to be a story but a plain statement of facts which actually occurred, and which I can remember after a lapse of fifteen years.

I have avoided as much as possible the gruesome and disgusting side of the war; these episodes are dim in my memory and thankfully forgotten. Such details can be found in nearly all war novels.

I never saw an officer drunk in action, nor did I have any of the unpleasant experiences which many authors of war books seem to have had, although I was in France for eighteen months.

Many of the gallant officers and men mentioned in this book were killed or have died since, so I hope this narrative will do something to perpetuate their memories.

Lastly, I would like to ¦thank General Sir Hubert Gough; The Director of the Committee of Imperial Defence (Historical Section); Major L. H. Cox and Mr. Kennedy Williamson, for their kind assistance.

WHITEHALL,

June, 1932.
SHREWSBURY.

INTRODUCTION

BY

GENERAL SIR HUBERT GOUGH, K.C.B., K.C.M.G.,

Commander of the 5th Army.

It is often said that people are tired of war books, but as the war fades into history the public, that awe-inspiring term for those at present inhabiting this country, is becoming less and less permeated by those who played any personal part in the Great War.

It is important, and surely it should be of absorbing interest to those who are too young to have been through those terrible days, to learn something of the spirit and characteristics of those who were called upon to live through them.

This story of a soldier's part in the war does not deal with profound questions of strategy, nor does it deal with the emotions, philosophical or more often sexual, which have been so much enlarged upon and exaggerated by some authors, but it does relate, in a cheery manner, the events of the daily life of a soldier in the war, of the hardships and great dangers which they faced daily.

In going through its pages a reader can see the unselfish, the cool, almost contented spirit with which the Englishman went through experiences completely foreign to his previous upbringing. It is interesting to note the wonderful adaptability of the race.

It is for these reasons that the present generation should read this book, which presents to them a picture quite different to anything they have experienced, and let us hope inspiring them with a resolution to maintain those solid foundations of the individual's character, which in the aggregate is the National character, and which was so greatly displayed by a previous generation.

HUBERT GOUGH.

71, Elm Park Gardens,
    London, S.W.10,
        August 21st, 1932.

TABLE OF CONTENTS.

ILLUSTRATIONS.

PROLOGUE.

July, 1914.

The Salle de Baccarat was crowded.

" Venez vous places Messieurs et Mesdames," called the Croupier.

I sat down in my seat.

People began to stroll back to the table.

"A vous, Monsieur," smiled the Croupier, pushing the shoe towards me.

I looked round.

A motley crowd : mostly elderly women, young girls from England looking on—some with anxious faces watching their husbands play—most of them looking as if they did not care if they won or lost. A typical pre-war crowd in France for a holiday. Jack called across from his seat, " Can I share your bank ? "

" Fifty francs only," I answered.

" Commencez, s'il vous plait," whispered the Croupier.

I tapped the ' shoe.'

" Banco ! " called a man on the other side of the Croupier.

I dealt the cards, not looking at mine.

" Carte ! " he cried.

Turning my cards up I saw to my delight that I held a knave and a nine.

" Neuf a la banque," called the Croupier.

" Suivi," called the man.

I dealt again. This time we both drew cards.

" Sept a la banque, le banque gagné," called the Croupier.

This was good.

" Banco " again. He wanted no cards this time ; he must have a six or a seven. I turned mine up—hurrah !—an eight.

" Huit, à la banque," called the Croupier.

There were now about 400 francs on the table. I glanced across at Jack : he was looking towards the ceiling with an air of supreme indifference.

" Banco " was called. This time by a man who had come up to the table from the outside.

" Shall I let it go ? " I called to Jack.

"As you like," he replied. " You are playing the cards."

I dealt him his two cards. He paused, looking at them.

" Non ! " he ejaculated.

I turned mine up—a seven and a five. Slowly I drew one from the shoe—a five—a natural.

" Huit, à la banque," called the Croupier. A crowd started to collect round the table. This was exciting. Outwardly I was quite cool, but inside I had a funny tight feeling.

" Marquez vos jeux," called the Croupier.

No one was prepared to go banco.

" Banco," called a voice in the distance : a little man came running up.

" Le main passe," I said at once. I was satisfied, I could not have stood the strain of another coup.

I left my seat to celebrate at the bar with Jack. There was the usual crowd there talking about nothing in particular.

The barman remarked " News from Russia pretty bad to-day."

" What's the matter, George ? " asked Jack.

" Oh, it will blow over like these things always do," scoffed another man.

" I'm not so sure," I said. " When I was walking to Boulogne to-day I saw a French battalion in full field kit going to the station. Personally I don't like the look of it—we are off to-morrow."

" I shan't go," replied Jack. " Nothing will stop us going back if there is a war."

We left the bar to stroll on the beach for half an hour before dinner. It was a lovely summer evening. The hotel at Wimereux was packed with holiday makers from England, and although there were rumours of war in the East, they did not worry.

Times were good, money was easy to earn—we were soft.

My wife was nervous. She had a premonition of bad times ahead. We had decided to return to England at lunch time that day.

The next day we departed, making the journey in comfort ; while my sister and her husband had a terrible time when they crossed a few days later.

The boats were packed with refugees.

I started as soon as I could to make things secure for my business in case of war. I had already telegraphed from France to my manager to buy flour, as a bakery business would feel the shortage at once if a war started—prices would rise.

I lived an uneventful life in those pre-war days, catching the 9 a.m. train from Weybridge, leaving my office at 5-30 p.m. to catch the 5-50 train at Waterloo—each day the same.

I did not go to town on Saturdays—played golf.

My life was similar to that of a thousand others. I was happy and contented.

The next four years were to shatter all that.

War was declared August 4th. I was in Piccadilly when the newspaper boys rushed into the Circus with the news. What a night ! London went mad with war fever.

All this time I was very unwell, but towards the end of August I was convalescent, so I applied to the War Office for a commission in the Yeomanry.

My brother-in-law Jack joined up at about the same time.

CHAPTER I.

WAR IN ENGLAND.

MY commission was gazetted in September.

Having purchased my uniform I left Weybridge for Shrewsbury, which was the headquarters of the newly-formed 2/1 Shropshire Yeomanry. I reported to the Adjutant, Captain Paul Young, the same evening.

Captain Young was a very smart and efficient officer who had lately retired from an Indian cavalry regiment. For a long time afterwards I was to remain very much in awe of him. An adjutant could be a very alarming person, as I quickly found out.

He told me I should be posted to ' B ' squadron, which was commanded by my uncle, Major C. T. Dugdale. The officers and men would do anything for him. He had a quick and impulsive temper. However, no one minded, as the storms quickly blew over.

The officers were billeted at the judge's lodgings, where Mr. and Mrs. Ward looked after our comforts for the next few months.

I found that with few exceptions my brother-officers knew about as little of soldiering as I did, so we spent the first few weeks drilling with the recruits, under the supervision of Regimental Sergt.-Major Leggatt and Sergt.-Major Bugg. As the regiment was a new one officers and men had to start from the beginning.

Equipment and uniforms were almost non-existent, so that most of the men wore plain clothes on parade.

We received a draft of Canadian horses just before Christmas, which caused great excitement. Many of these horses were wild and unbroken, so the services of those who were accustomed to breaking horses were in great demand.

We took them out to try on the racecourse, with Captain Prestage in command, one morning. One particular horse was a great nuisance, as none of the men could stay on its back, so Captain Prestage decided to try the horse himself in private.

With two men he took the creature behind a high wooden wall where we could not see what was going on. We awaited the result with interest.

Before very long his head appeared above the wall quickly three times—and then disappeared.

The horse was then led home for training in the riding school.

We all had to go through a course of riding at the school, under the regimental sergeant-major. He made us ride round the ring bare back for an hour each day until we ached in every joint. I could not sit down with any comfort for a week.

None of us will ever forget the great occasion in the riding school when Captain Evans, who was a well-known rider to hounds, placed his right foot in the stirrup when the instructor gave the word of command " prepare to mount."

The horses were a great joy as each officer was responsible for about twenty-eight, which were billeted in stable yards all over the town. We rapidly made progress with our drill, and by the end of February, 1915, we could drill by squadrons fairly efficiently.

The rivalry between the squadrons was intense.

'A' squadron was commanded by Major George Onslow, who was a great horse master and a superb horseman. He believed in keeping his horses fit and in hard condition. We thought privately that they needed clipping.

My uncle believed in plenty of food for the horses, and plenty of flesh on them. They were groomed till they shone. My troop was particularly well favoured, as I bought extra rations for them myself. My knowledge of horses was small, but we pulled one through a bad attack of pneumonia by good nursing and giving it doses of medicine, which I read about in a book.

' C ' squadron was led by Major R. C. B. Partridge, with Captain Evans as his second in command. Both these officers were very thin men, so their horses were thin too, which caused much ribald commentary from Heathcote, of ' B ' squadron. However, both Partridge and Evans were fine judges, and their horses were always fit.

Soon after the new year Colonel C. U. Corbett left us and Lord Forester took over command of the regiment.

In the spring of 1915 we received orders that we should go into brigade camp at Lambton Park, in Durham. We had not been there long when we came into contact with the war for the first time.

One night I was woken up by an explosion—two more followed. I dressed quickly to find the officers collected in the mess. Orders were given for all the troops to lead their horses into the avenue at the edge of the Park. Here we waited till 1 a.m., when we returned to camp. We could hear bombs dropping near Newcastle, and we were told afterwards that a Zeppelin had raided Palmers' Works, doing considerable damage.

During the time we were at Lambton Park we trained hard —field days in the country, shooting at the range, and finally brigade drill, which was excellent fun.

We left the brigade camp late in the summer to take over coast defence, just north of Newbiggin. Our regiment was responsible for guarding Druridge Bay, which was supposed to be the best landing beach in the north of England. Our camp was at Ellington.

Ellington Camp was situated in a bleak spot not more than a mile from the sea. However, we were fairly comfortable in tents when it was fine, but during wet and cold weather we were miserable, as there was nothing to do.

It was the duty of the patrol officer to ride round the posts in Druridge Bay each night at different hours.

Our days were spent in squadron and regimental drill, and in trench digging on the dunes. This was a most disheartening job, as the sand filled them in again almost as soon as they were completed.

On one occasion when I was patrol officer I decided to visit the posts just before dawn, so I started off with Roberts, my mounted orderly, at 4 a.m. When we reached the post at the far end of Druridge Bay we found the men in charge of the post on the shore watching a large round object which was being swept ashore on the incoming tide. I dismounted and sent Roberts with the horses into the dunes.

Soon the thing reached the shore and stuck as the tide began to recede. We were then able to make a closer examination.

It was a round iron ball, about four feet high, with some sort of machinery at one end. We approached it with considerable caution.

One of the men, braver than the rest, went quite close to it. Suddenly he turned and ran for his life shouting, " It's smoking, Sir—it's a mine—run for it."

My word, we ran like hares for the shelter of the dunes.

The thing then began to smoke freely. Every minute we expected a terrific explosion. It smoked and smoked, until suddenly it burst into flame. It then dawned on me that it was a phosphorus buoy which they used for the submarine nets.

We rode home feeling rather small to relate the great adventure to the mess.

One day the Colonel mentioned quite casually at lunch that the Sergeant-Major had reported that there was trouble with the chimney of the officers' mess kitchen. My uncle at once took notice. All his instincts for putting things right himself were aroused. Privately, he decided to do the job himself that afternoon, and what is more, he did it, and thoroughly.

The matter was discussed in the sergeants' mess that night, and the veterans then decided that a precedent had been established for army records. Such a thing had never been done by the second-in-command of a regiment before.

Worse was to follow a few days later. The Colonel had mentioned that he had seen bits of paper blowing about the camp. At once the Major sent for the Sergeant-Major, telling him to order ' B ' squadron to parade dismounted at 2-30 p.m.

The squadron, complete with officers, cleared the camp of waste paper, marching through the camp in line of troops. Yet another precedent had been established.

The days passed happily. We enjoyed life—so far we had seen little of the war.

In November we moved to the town of Newbiggin, into billets.

It was a cold bleak place, and there was very little to do outside our ordinary daily work, but we spent many cheery nights in Newcastle.

The spring arrived and with it all kinds of rumours about a threatened rebellion in Ireland, and at that time we received secret information from headquarters about a projected enemy landing in the north of England.

Our defences in Druridge Bay and Newbiggin were complete, while elaborate arrangements were in existence for instant action in case of emergency; furthermore, the civilian population had received minute instructions as to their movements if the threatened landing should take place. They were ordered to proceed to the rear by specified routes, passing through fields near the roads, which were to be used exclusively by the military. Roger Barber Starkey was responsible for their evacuation.

At this time our Adjutant attended a staff meeting, at which all the plans to meet an invasion went through a dress rehearsal.

The Zeppelin raids on Newcastle grew more frequent as the weather improved. Apparently they used Newbiggin Point as a guide, as they invariably came over us on their way to Newcastle, returning the same way. They had an unpleasant habit of throwing overboard, near us, any bombs they had not dropped in Newcastle. I suppose they considered they would be wasted if dropped in the North Sea. Sometimes these bombs fell within half a mile, exploding with terrific force, alarming my wife and children considerably.

In April our Adjutant left us, and Colonel Lord Forester appointed me to take his place, as I had been assistant Adjutant for some weeks.

The activity at sea was of great interest, as apparently German submarines were frequently sighted off our coast.

One fine Saturday afternoon, while playing golf, my opponent and I had stopped to watch one of our newly-built destroyers passing the point, quite close in shore, when suddenly we heard a gun fire at sea. We heard the whistle of a shell, which to our amazement dropped with a big splash in the sea quite close to the destroyer. In the far distance we thought we could see a submarine on the surface.

Clouds of smoke shot from the funnels of the destroyer as she turned to go in pursuit. Three more shells followed. The destroyer opened fire, and under forced draught tore out to sea.

Needless to say we never heard the result of this encounter. The navy were a very reticent crowd.

The activities at sea were always interesting and mysterious. One fine morning we saw a quantity of small trawlers working in Newbiggin Bay. They appeared to be laying some kind of net across the entrance. At frequent intervals they left buoys to mark its position. They completed the work during the day, leaving about three trawlers to guard the net by night.

Nothing much happened for two days, when in the early morning we saw a small fleet in the bay hard at work—peculiar-looking craft with big cranes at one end were busily working near the net. We had no idea what they were doing until they landed their fish—it was a submarine caught in the net. They towed it to Newcastle, where they found all the crew dead inside. The submarine was undamaged.

We could not help feeling sorry for the Germans who, while hiding on the bottom of the bay, had been trapped by the nets. They were caught and entangled as they attempted to escape —an awful death.

At the beginning of May we heard from brigade head-quarters that the War Office expected a serious attempt would be made by the enemy to effect a landing on our part of the coast within the next few days, so orders were given for our men to 'stand to' each night. The Secret Plans, known as 'Scheme G,' were explained to all concerned. These especially applied to the civilian population.

We decided to send our wives and children away at this time, until the situation became more calm.

On May 7th, at 8 p.m., a message came through stating that six Zeppelins had been sighted proceeding in our direction. At the same time the word 'prepare' in code reached us. Word was at once sent to the Colonel, who was dining at Seaton.

This message was the first part of 'Scheme G.'

Immediately orders were given to squadrons to 'stand to.' Transport was loaded with the small amount of baggage we could take with us. All eyes were turned towards the sea, peering into the darkness for the first sign of the enemy.

At 10 p.m., when all our arrangements were complete, a message was flashed through from our squadron in Druridge Bay to inform us that a bomb had dropped north of them.

Soon after this I left the orderly room to snatch a few hours' sleep in my clothes. I suppose I had been asleep for two hours—semi-consciously I heard a noise—stirring restlessly on the sofa half-awake—the noise was repeated—this time the bell rang continuously. Fully awake now, I rushed to the window in the darkened room to see who had roused me at this time of night—1-30 a.m.

From my window on the first floor I could see the sea lit by search-lights, their beams flashing far out to sea. In the distance I could hear the dull booming of guns.

I rushed downstairs.

An orderly handed me a message. Glancing at it I saw it was in code.

Waiting to collect my revolver and the rest of my kit I locked the door of the house and ran to the orderly room. Opening the safe I soon decoded the message, which ran as follows :—

" Heavy bombardment south. Enemy fleet accompanied by transports proceeding north. Adopt Scheme G."

It had come.

Messages were despatched to the Colonel and to the squadron leaders. The Colonel arrived.

" Order all squadrons to saddle up in stables leaving one man in four to look after the horses.

" Transport to leave at once for first halting place and await orders.

" One limbered wagon to come here to load regimental headquarters and proceed to first halting place. The rest of the regiment to man trenches.

" The civilians need not be evacuated yet, but inform the police."

Within an hour all orders had been carried out. Meanwhile we could hear guns booming in the distance and the search-lights swept the horizon.

We waited in suspense.

An hour passed. We could no longer hear the guns. Another hour—the first signs of dawn appeared in the east.

The telephone bell startled us all. I heard a voice in the distance : " Cancel Scheme G. Confirming this by motor-cycle messenger."

A false alarm.

The tension broke—refreshment was indicated and promptly produced. The transport was recalled, the police informed, saddles and bridles removed, but we still ' stood to ' till daylight appeared.

Was it a false alarm ? The message was definite.

We were told afterwards that the information was true, and that the transports turned back, their fleet going on to bombard the Hartlepools. This accounted for the gun fire we had heard.

My wife and children returned from Carlisle. Life settled down again to the ordinary routine.

Soon afterwards we left our billets, but we had our last thrill before we left.

We had received reports from our posts that mysterious lights had been seen at night flashing out to sea.

One night we received a message stating that signals were now flashing from a house in a row at the end of the town.

Quickly collecting another officer and a party of men armed to the teeth we proceeded to the spot, first sending three cyclists to see that no one left the house. When we arrived I ordered the men to surround the house, which was in total darkness. We conversed in hoarse whispers. Two of us approached the house with great caution.

I knocked on the door.

A window was thrown open.

" Who the hell are you ? " called a man with a rough voice, very English.

" Come down and open the door," I replied. " We want to search the house."

" What the —— for ? " he shouted.

" Oh, George, what is it ? " cried a woman.

" Soldiers ! " he muttered.

I was getting impatient.

" We shall break down the door if you don't open."

" All right.   I am coming," he growled.

We searched the house from top to bottom.   The man could not make out what was the matter.   We found a lamp in the first floor room which was still warm.   We questioned him closely.   He said he had kept the blind down all the evening.

I suspected it was another false alarm.

We gave him a serious talking to about showing a light. He was very alarmed, but I am sure quite innocent of signalling to enemy submarines.

We decided to go home.

Soon afterwards the regiment moved from billets into camp near Woodhorn, where once more brigade training started.

Sandford had been appointed bombing officer, with instructions to teach the regiment the mysteries of Mills bombs and rifle grenades.

His bombing class of advanced pupils was held on the sand dunes by the sea.

One day General Little sent a message through to say he would inspect the bombing class at work that afternoon, so Sandford was aroused to feverish activity to show the Colonel how well his bombers could do their job.   He thought that it would be a brilliant idea to erect a stout wooden stake in front of the bombing trench, to give the bomb throwers the direction.

The General and his staff, accompanied by the Colonel, were duly placed in the trench to watch with interest the excellent target practice the men made, when, to the horror of them all, one of the men hit the direction post with his live bomb, which bounced back into the trench where the General and his staff were standing.   Panic ensued.   Everyone bolted for their lives, some fell down.   It was a most undignified retreat, but no one was hurt.

The General was perfectly furious.

About this time ugly rumours began to be whispered abroad that we were to lose our horses and be remounted on push bikes.   Alas !   It was only too true, as orders came through for me to go on a cycle course.

When I returned the Colonel gave orders that all officers were to go through a course of riding school on push bikes under my instruction.

It is impossible for me to describe this push bike riding school. I can only leave it to the imagination of my readers. I could only stand about three-quarters of an hour of it, otherwise I should have had hysterics.

Later on the regiment was mounted on ' push bikes,' which made it difficult for the senior N.C.O's to uphold their dignity.

However, we all enjoyed life thoroughly, although it was a heavy blow to lose our horses.

Shortly we were to send our first draft to France without officers, but Partridge, Ingleby, Stanier and myself received orders to follow them later.

CHAPTER II.

I PROCEED OVERSEAS.

OUR first draft left Newbiggin for France at the end of July, 1916, being distributed amongst the K.S.L.I. battalions.

hey arrived in time to take part in the battle of Guillemont in September, where they earned much praise from the Colonel of the 6th K.S.L.I.

We received our marching orders in September, sailing at night from Southampton.

As the ship entered the harbour at Havre, after a fair crossing, it was just growing light. Slowly we moved to the quayside, all of us looking over the side.

Here was war at last.

Rows of new guns, limbers, G.S. wagons, etc., were lined up ready to be taken up to the battle area by train.

We were told to show our passes to the landing officer, who ordered us to report at once to No. 2 Infantry Base Lepot, which lay outside the town.

Chartering a dilapidated cab we all piled in with our kits to drive through the cobbled streets of the old town and up the hill behind it to the depot.

The depot was a huge hutment camp in charge of a commandant.

We reported our arrival at once and were allotted to a large hut with about ten other officers. We were told we should remain here for a few days to go through the gas chamber test before we were despatched up to the front to join our battalions.

He informed us that Stanier, Ingleby and myself were posted to the 6th K.S.L.I., who were near Amiens in billets.

We attended parade each day, where we were initiated into the mysteries of infantry drill, of which we were entirely ignorant, being yeomen.

We went through the gas chamber without harm.

Our marching orders having arrived we walked to the station, arriving in good time for the train, which was due to start at 8 p.m. The train was in, so we dumped our kits in a first-class carriage, hoping that we should have it to ourselves.

The gloomy station was full of troops weighed down with full marching equipment.

There was a wonderful canteen run by ladies, where one could obtain anything from a hot meal to a packet of cigarettes. We purchased sandwiches and some magazines to pass the time away during the journey.

The train pulled out of the station at 9 p.m., slowly crawling along about ten miles per hour.

We alternately talked and slept. The train halted, for no apparent reason ; we could only suppose that the steam in the engine gave out.

The next morning the train halted in a large junction called Rome's Camp. Here we had some tea made from hot water from the engine.

After a stop of about three hours we started again at an even slower rate, as there was a long train in front of us and another behind. At last we arrived at a station where the railway transport officer told us to go to Picquigny, where our battalion was billeted.

We walked through the village to battalion headquarters, curious glances following us. We felt like new boys arriving at school for the first time.

Colonel Wood was charming : we were soon at our ease with him. He told us that the draft he had received from our regiment had done well, and that he hoped we should be very happy while we were with the 6th K.S.L.I.

Colonel E. A. Wood was a man of ample proportions and perfectly dressed, a large bandanna silk handkerchief stuck out of his breast pocket. Afterwards I found that he carried an alpenstock when going round the line and an electric torch, which he used on every possible occasion, much to the horror of those who were with him. He was utterly devoid of fear or nerves.

I was posted to ' D ' Company.

Leaving battalion headquarters I went across the street to a villa, which was ' D ' Company headquarters. Here Captain McKimm introduced himself and the other officers.

They were all very young, eighteen to twenty-one years old. McKimm was a large man with frizzy red hair. I found out afterwards that he was not given to talking much, but when he did so his remarks were very much to the point. On all occasions he was perfectly calm. All the junior officers under him were second Lieutenants, while I was a full Lieutenant. This was distinctly awkward, as I had no active service experience. These boys were all war veterans.

At this time Jack Whittingham was appointed to be my orderly and officer's servant. He was a very good looking young man with a weakness for the fair sex and a beautiful smile. He accompanied me wherever I went, and always remained cheerful, no matter what the circumstances were.

I found that the Company officers were very pleasant, but not exactly affable, as they realised I was their senior officer without front line experience. Naturally they were rather inclined to resent a novice. Later on the situation became almost unbearable, so much so that I went to see the Colonel to find out what my position with the Company was. He soon cleared the air and all was well once more.

Tim Stanier and I shared a most comfortable billet. By this time we had become great friends, although he was years younger than I was. He was always game for anything—a most cheery soul.

Soon afterwards Hubert Ingleby left us to go to the gunners. We both missed him very much as he had a great gift of repartee.

I soon settled down to the routine, but my ignorance of infantry drill was a great handicap. Luckily most of the men in our Company were ex-yeomen, so they understood me when I shouted " sections right " when I meant " fours right."

The Company Sergeant-Major did his best to help by standing at my side whispering the words of command that were necessary. After a week or so we were ordered to move nearer to the line, so leaving our comfortable billets with great regret we proceeded by route march to Meaulte, sending Kimpster ahead to prepare for our arrival. Kimpster was a priceless lad of eighteen, with a pink face and a perpetual smile. He did not know the meaning of the word ' nerves.'

It was a dreadful day, pouring with rain, so we arrived tired out and soaked to the skin, to find the camp was not ready and that no hot food had been prepared for us. There was a big to do while we waited with the troops in the rain. Finally we managed to get the men settled in fairly comfortably. It turned out that Kimpster had found no one at the camp when he arrived, so he proceeded to get in touch with Corps headquarters by telephone, telling them exactly what he thought of them. This brought a young officer at once on horseback with an orderly. He was most apologetic, telling Kimpster that he would see to the matter himself at once. Kimpster was a youth who spoke his mind, so he told this officer exactly what he thought of the muddle and a good deal more besides. Things were quickly put right, but the incident caused much amusement when it came out that the staff officer was His Royal Highness the Prince of Wales.

For a long time afterwards Kimpster kept trying to recall all the words he had said to him.

This camp was situated just behind the original front line of July 1st, 1916. For several weeks the battalion was employed on road work, while I attended a Lewis gun school at Meaulte.

Soon after my return we moved into a camp nearer the line at Carnoy.

CHAPTER III.

UNDER INSTRUCTION.

THE hutment camp at Carnoy in November, 1916, was a most depressing place. Little remained of the village except heaps of rubbish, which gave no idea of the houses which once had stood there. The church and the town hall had vanished, only piles of brick remained.

All this was a new experience for me. We were now on the old battlefield of the Somme, which had been the scene of fierce fighting a few months before.

Ceaseless activity went on day and night—transport, limbers, lorries passing through made sleep difficult. We worked on the roads all day.

The thunder of the guns in front of us made me realise that soon I should have to take my turn in the trenches. I sometimes wondered what it would be like. However, I had little time for thought, my mind was kept occupied by the work in hand—just as well.

One night the Adjutant sent for me.

Leaving our company hut I walked across to battalion headquarters, where I found Colonel Wood and the Adjutant alone.

"Your time has come," laughed the Colonel. "We have orders here from brigade that you are to report for instruction to a battalion of the Middlesex regiment at Guillemont to-morrow. I want to give you a few hints. Remember you will have no responsibility, as you are only going for the experience. There will be no need for you to do anything except keep your eyes open. You will be under shell fire, of course," he continued. "Don't be afraid to duck when you hear a shell coming; we all do. Don't put your head over the top in the front line—it might get hit."

He got up to say good-bye, adding : "I expect you will enjoy it, as it will be a new experience. Good luck to you."

Starting off the next afternoon in full battle equipment, I walked up the road towards Trones Wood, which was the scene of severe fighting in September. I found little remaining of the wood except stumps of shell-torn trees. I then bore to my right, as the direction post there indicated " Guillemont half a mile."

The village was even more dilapidated than Carnoy, and it was difficult to find any trace of it. On making enquiries I was directed to an old quarry, where I found the battalion of the Middlesex regiment, with whom I was to gain my first experience of the war, and a very cheery crowd they were.

I was told to report to the Adjutant, who had a dug-out in the side of the quarry. He got up to shake hands, remarking, " Delighted to see you. I hope we shall be able to show you to-night how a relief should be done. All you have to do is to look on and stick to the company commander like glue. We start from here at eight, so it would be best if you reported to 'A' company now, as they will be having some food, and you must get a good meal inside you before you start. Good luck."

'A' company headquarters was in a hut just outside the quarry, near a silent battery of howitzers, which they told me were 9.2's. The company officers were all at mess, and evidently expecting me, as they made me join them in an excellent meal, washed down with whiskey and water.

They did their best to pass the time by giving me hints, and some of them were good ones, as I found out later.

Without any warning the howitzer battery outside opened fire. I nearly jumped out of my seat, much to the amusement of the others. They were accustomed to it.

The company moved off at 8 p.m. to the minute, the company commander in front, with me by his side. I noticed that there were quite big gaps between each platoon. The Captain explained, " We have to pass Ginchy Corner, which they shell pretty often, and we don't want the men too thick on the ground. There it is, over there ! " He indicated the remains of a shed with a few trees about three hundred yards ahead.

"A shell or two will arrive before we get there."

Just then I heard what I took to be an express train coming towards us—louder and louder—till there was a shriek and a loud explosion as the shell landed, throwing up clouds of smoke and debris.

" We shall just about get there before the next one arrives if we hurry a bit," remarked the Captain. " Let us get a move on."

As we reached the place he shouted : " Get down quick, here comes another ! "

A howling noise, quickly turning to a shriek ; with a roar it exploded fifty yards to my right. I had forgotten to duck.

" You damned fool ! " the Captain shouted. Keep your —— head down. We don't want you a casualty yet. Come on before another one arrives."

I felt a fool and privately made up my mind he would not have to remind me again to keep my head down. I had thought it was " not the thing to do " to duck.

Leaving Ginchy we walked down a rough track on which they had laid duckboards. Many of these were broken, causing much bad language from the troops who were following behind.

The Captain pointed ahead to what appeared to be the beginning of a drain, remarking :

" We go down that communication trench about a mile, as we are on the top of the ridge. Personally I would prefer to go along the top, but we cannot walk along the sky line in such numbers."

The trench was quite eight feet deep and quite dry, as the weather had not yet broken.

I followed the Captain, tripping up over broken duckboards, as it was now quite dark. We seemed to have walked miles, but in reality it was much less.

When we reached the end he turned to me, talking in a low voice.

" We have to go across the open now, and there appear to be no guides here. I shall have to try to find out which way to go."

He left me. I watched with great curiosity the star shells going up in front from both the enemy lines and our own ; these lights appeared to be only half a mile away from us.

Meanwhile the company had left the communication trench ; I could hear the jingle of their equipment but could not see them.

About a quarter of an hour passed.

Suddenly the Captain reappeared out of the darkness.

" Follow me," he murmured. " There are no guides, but I have a rough idea where the line is."

We followed in a string, one behind the other. A few shells whined over from our guns to fall behind the German lines. Verey lights rose from the front, lighting up the shell-scarred country for a few seconds. There was a sickly smell of decay in the air.

We halted again. Once more the Captain went in search of the guides who were supposed to have met us. Meanwhile we stood still.

I suppose we had wandered for about two hours when we sighted another party of men between ourselves and the line. The Captain led us towards them.

" Who are you ? " he challenged.

" Middlesex ' C ' Company," they replied. They were one of our companies, lost as well.

Things began to look serious. Luckily my lack of experience prevented me from knowing how grave our position was. Here were two companies wandering about not far behind the front line, liable to be seen at any time by the enemy.

Shells began to fall near us—5.9's someone said. Things began to look dangerous ; the Captain had to decide something.

" Pass the word down the line to follow me," he whispered. " I am going to get the men into some sort of trench. We shall be spotted any minute now."

Without any warning a rocket went up immediately in front, revealing us quite clearly.

" Golden rain, the Bosches S.O.S.," muttered the Captain. " Now we are in for it."

Silence for about a minute while we hurried towards the trench. Should we get there in time ?

Flashes appeared all along the front behind the German line ; a noise like drums being beaten rapidly in the distance— shells screamed over us to fall fifty yards behind us—more rockets were sent up from the line—pandemonium broke loose. Shells were howling, screaming, crashing all around us : the air was full of smoke, chips of shell whistled through the

air—the noise was stupendous. We ran towards the trench.
I stumbled into a deep hole on to my head—lay there panting
for breath. A shell dropped ten yards away covering me with
earth. I could not see. Getting up I leant against the back of
the trench, for trench it was. I was not afraid, I was past
that. The Germans seemed to have the range of the trench
exactly, shells were falling in hundreds. I could not hear or
see anything. With my hands over my head I hugged the
wall of the trench ; with a crash a shell dropped in the trench
I was in. Struggling from the earth it threw up I moved as
far as I could to the right. A screaming roar—crash—right
on to the parapet in front of my head—the blast blew off my
tin hat, throwing me to the bottom of the trench. I thought
my last hour had come. I was inclined to panic—I was alone—
where were the others ?

The shelling slackened, moving along the trench to the
right. I was challenged in French. A French officer
approached.

" Who are you ? " he asked in English.

" Attached to the Middlesex regiment," I replied.

" Do you know where they are ? " he asked.

" No," I answered. " We have been lost in the open for
two hours, but I expect we shall find them back there."

" You have had a pretty rough time," he remarked. " Will
you take me along with you ? I must tell your C.O. that there
is a gap between us of at least two hundred yards."

We chatted about England as we walked.

" Were you at the Varsity ? " he asked.

" Yes. I was at Oxford, Hertford College," I replied.

" I was at the House," he cried. " Went down in 1909."

" What an amazing thing," I said. " That is the year I
went down, too."

We talked of Oxford standing there in the trench, war
forgotten.

" My word," he cried. " We must get on, as I have to find
that battalion of yours."

We found them at last.

The Company Commander recognised me.

" Who is your friend ? " he asked.

I replied, " This French officer met me lower down. He says there is a gap of two hundred yards between your men and his."

" By jove ! " he cried. " That is pretty bad."

" Come with me, Sir," he added. " We must go to see the Colonel."

They left me to explore.

I met a man who told me that one of our machine gun posts had been hit by a shell, and that most of the crew had been killed. The man who survived told me about it.

" It was like this, Sir," he said. " We had got the gun on the parapet when we heard a shell coming right at us. I dropped to the bottom of the trench. The shell hit the gun, knocking all the others on to the top of me ; they saved my life."

The trench here was a shambles.

The men, however, who were not hit, seemed to be going about as if nothing unusual had happened.

I ventured to ask a sergeant if this sort of thing happened every night. When he saw who I was he became quite communicative.

" Good gracious, no Sir," he laughed. " You have been damned unlucky. That there barrage put the wind up me proper—the worst I have seen since the Somme—whizz bangs, 5.9's and big stuff coming over like hot cakes, weren't they ? Never mind, Sir, you can rest assured you won't see much worse while you are out here."

I was frightfully pleased and replied : " Oh, sergeant, I am so glad to hear someone else was alarmed ; personally I was terrified."

He roared with laughter.

" You will get on all right, Sir," he said, " if you can stick that little show."

He thankfully took a pull at my flask. We smoked cigarettes.

He told me a few things.

" We all get the wind up, Sir, but we try not to let the troops know. Take my tip, Sir, I am older than you are—

don't try to be too —— brave. Only do what you are told ;
be cautious. Some of these 'ere officers chuck their lives
away : damn fine fellows they are, too ; we can't afford to lose
them. Who is to take their places ? "

I rose to return to company headquarters, and held out
my hand to wish him good-bye.

" Good luck, Sir," he said. " Remember what I have
said."

I never forgot this advice, and I believe he was responsible
for my survival.

The night passed without further incident worth relating,
and during this period I succeeded in getting some sleep.

At the first sign of daylight the Captain woke up.

" Stand to now," he yawned. " You will have to reach the
communication trench before daylight. Get hold of a cup of
tea and push off. Good luck to you. Sorry you have had such
an exciting night."

I climbed gingerly out of the trench. It was hardly light
enough to see anything. Verey lights occasionally lit up the
ground on all sides ; it was ominously quiet. Occasional bursts
of machine gun fire shattered the silence ; guns flashed in the
distance, the shells moaning over to drop with a crump behind
me. The early morning freshness was spoilt by the smell of
explosive and decaying flesh.

I started to run back, dodging shell holes and other
obstructions.

A sniper fired, I could hear the bullet sing past me. I ran
on ; he fired again, nearer this time. I dropped down, crawled
a few yards, rose to run again ; it was lighter, I could see the
entrance to the communication trench. Once again he fired,
the bullet hitting a tree in front of me with a ' plop.' I was
frightened and dropped again into a shell hole. Looking up
I could see the line I had left and the German wire. It was
too light. I decided to make one last wild rush ; the sniper
might have got tired of waiting, as I had been at least ten
minutes in the shell hole. I scrambled out and bolted as hard
as I could run for the shelter of the trench.

Safety at last. I lay down panting for breath.

I arrived back during the morning at our battalion headquarters, where I related my experiences to the others.   They
roared with laughter, evidently thinking it a huge joke.

A few days later we went into the line ourselves.

CHAPTER IV.

Mud.

PLATOON by platoon the company tramped down the muddy road towards Guillemont. It was pouring with rain, the night was as black as pitch. Towards the front, star shells rose and fell in the distance. Our guns in front occasionally fired a salvo.

Following in the rear of the last platoon I wondered how long we should take to reach our destination opposite Les Boeufs. The men in front simply crawled. Passing Guillemont the 9.2 battery opened fire, the shells shrieking away into the distance, probably to fall amongst some enemy party going into the line like ourselves.

Approaching Ginchy Corner the men in front of us quickened their pace ; evidently they were aware of its evil reputation. I longed to run.

When still one hundred yards distant we heard the shells coming. All the men dropped ; I did the same. It was dark and I was behind them. We hurried on, another salvo would arrive in three minutes. The enemy kept to a strict time table.

After Ginchy the pace slowed down once more. We were moving towards the top of a low ridge on duckboard tracks : lights in a dugout on our left indicated the whereabouts of a first field dressing station. The men in front of me seemed to move faster ; someone in front tripped up and fell, his heavy equipment clattering. Men shouted for those in front to go slower.

A battery of field guns fired a salvo just behind us. We were so close we could feel the blast, most nerve shattering.

We tried to hurry when we reached the top of the ridge ; it was an unhealthy spot. The duckboard track was very much damaged ; shell holes had to be avoided. The track became more undefined.

The sergeant-major said that the communication trench was not far away. We staggered on, slipping and cursing. Frequently men fell into the shell holes : we were all covered with mud and wet through. The pace was now a mere crawl, the mud was almost up to our knees. A man fell out exhausted. What was to be done?

Telling the sergeant-major to go on, I waited with him. Tebby, one of the signallers, remained to help me. The others disappeared into the darkness.

The man was beat, panting for breath, the sweat pouring from him. He was an oldish man. After a pull from my flask he revived sufficiently to allow him to stagger along after the others ; squelching through the mud we followed. We hustled him along, holding him up by the arms. Not a sign of the company could we see or hear.

After a quarter of an hour we halted.

" Better wait here, Sir," said Tebby. " They will come to find us."

The effort of pulling this man along through the mud had exhausted us both. I had to decide whether to leave him and go on with Tebby, or stay with him. Presently we heard steps approaching. A figure loomed up in the darkness revealing McKimm himself, who had returned to find me. Waiting for the company to enter the communication trench he had noticed that I was not in my place in the rear.

" What is all this about ? " he asked. " What's the matter with him ? " indicating the man.

" He's beat. Says he can't walk another yard," I replied.

" Come on," he said to the man, without further comment. The man laboriously rose to his feet and walked on.

The communication trench was full of water up to our thighs. We decided to walk on the top as it was quiet. The rain poured down pitilessly. In front of us we could see a small rise, beyond it the Verey lights rose and fell. There was a fœtid stench in the air, unburied bodies lay on each side. We struggled on almost exhausted, wrenching our legs out of the clinging mud. At last we came to the rise. We had been walking for hours ; we entered the communication trench again. We were close to the line ; over the rise were the front line trenches, only fifty yards from the enemy in places.

Some men directed us to the company headquarters in a dugout. McKimm and I slithered down uneven steps plastered with mud. At the bottom we found a room lit with candles. The air was stuffy but warm.

"Where the hell have you been ? " someone said. " Got lost or something ? "

" Have a drink ? "

Whiskey and water impregnated with chlorate of lime helped to revive us.

Suddenly I leapt to my feet with a yell of pain. Cramp in the thighs. They quickly pulled off my mud-soaked breeches. One man rubbed each leg as hard as he could ; the precious whiskey was used as an embrocation. Soon the massage eased the agony. I was in a pretty bad state : it was suggested I should go back. I decided to stay.

As my first turn for duty in the line was not due for a few hours I ate some bully beef and bread and butter, and then went to sleep.

A few hours' sleep revived me. I awoke at 5 a.m.

In half an hour I was due to relieve Simon in the front line. Whittingham produced hot bacon and tea, which did me good. I no longer noticed my wet clothes.

The others were still asleep as I crawled up the stairs in the dark ; pulling aside the filthy blanket which covered the entrance I found that day was breaking.

Alone I walked along the trench, knee deep in mud, for about fifty yards. The support trench now lay at right angles. Here were groups of men huddled together against the side of the trench for what little warmth they could obtain from each other, their ground sheets over their shoulders, rifles propped up by their sides.

Further on I took a turning where I found myself in the front line trench. Walking along it as best I could I found sentry posts, the sentry watching through a periscope. Under a primitive shelter cut into the parapet I found Simon.

" Thank God you have come," he yawned. " Stand to in a quarter of an hour. It has been pretty quiet. So-long ! " He departed.

The men were stirring. It was now nearly 6 a.m.

At ' stand-to ' I went along my platoon front with the sergeant to inspect the men and their rifles. The men looked blue with cold, they were wet through. Hot tea with rum was served out after " stand down."

The morning's work began. The trench in places had fallen in during the night ; this had to be put in order. Water was bailed out and everyone worked hard to make things more comfortable.

I visited the men holding a sap pushed forward from our trench to within fifty yards of the enemy. Only a shallow cutting led to this, so I had to wriggle and crawl through the mud to reach it. They said they had passed a quiet night. Another man then arrived with their rations.

The call of nature was urgent—the sap cut out at the back of the trench for the purpose was exposed—I imagined I was in full view of the enemy. A sniper's bullet sang past. I could see in front of the enemy wire.

Returning to the trench I found the men hard at work. Time passed monotonously. I was relieved—had some food in the dugout, bully, bread and butter, tinned apricots.

I slept a little, then read for a while. Soon I should have to go on duty again.

The night passed without incident. There was a little shelling but they fell behind us.

The weather was too dreadful for much activity on either side.

Another monotonous day passed. We were to be relieved that night. Human nature could not stand more than forty-eight hours under such conditions. At 7-30 p.m. we were ready to struggle back to our billets. The primus stove in its biscuit box had to be carried by someone—Whittingham volunteered.

The relieving company arrived quite exhausted. Their officers took over from us. The company left platoon by platoon by the communication trench ; only the sergeant-major and myself remained.

After a look round for stragglers we departed, soon catching up Whittingham in the communication trench struggling along with the primus stove. We took it in turns to carry it.

On leaving the trench we saw a man stuck in a shell hole.

" Give us a hand, mate. I can't move in this —— mud." he shouted.

It took two of us, one on each arm, to move him at all.

" Something's caught," he yelled.

Just then he came away from the mud causing us to fall over.

We roared with laughter. Poor devil. He had left his breeches, pants, and everything else in the mud ; he stood in his shirt.

" What are you going to do now ? " laughed the sergeant-major.

" Don't you worry about me, Sir," he replied. I shall get back to billets if I have to crawl the whole —— way ! "

We waited a little while to see him start, and as he appeared to be going well we left him.

It was pitch dark and still raining. The mud seemed to be worse than ever, but we were going out of the line. The thought of this spurred us on. The primus stove, however, got heavier and heavier.

Just over the ridge we stopped to examine a man who was apparently dead.

The sergeant-major shook him. He groaned.

" What's up ? " he asked. "Are you hit ? "

The man looked up.

" I am beat," he muttered. " Can't go another yard."

" Come on," I said. " You must pull yourself together. We are all beat. Get up, we will help you."

He groaned again.

The sergeant-major's temper was somewhat frayed. The man was a corporal.

We helped him to his feet, gave him a drink from my flask. He collapsed again. He was a big man and we were exhausted. He fell face downwards in the mud.

Once more the three of us dragged him to his feet, pulling him a few yards.

" You remain here. I will get some stretcher bearers for you," I told him.

We left him with his head on the duckboards.

He had gone when the stretcher bearers came for him.

At last we reached Guillemont to find the field kitchen. Hot tea and rum worked wonders. It did not take us long to reach Carnoy.

By the time we arrived the others had seen to the comforts of the men and were sitting down to a good meal. I was glad to join them.

Tired as I was I managed to have a hot bath, using very strong and expensive violet toilet soap. I required some sweet smelling soap as a contrast to the odours of the line, and then into soft silk pyjamas and a warm ' flea bag."

We slept late.

The battalion paraded the next day for medical inspection and baths. The cases of trench feet were numerous ; nearly two hundred men were sent to hospital. Poor devils, some of them were in great pain.

The battalion only suffered two casualties from wounds.

The weather was atrocious ; troops could only remain for forty-eight hours at a time in the line. This continued until December 23rd, when we were relieved.

Christmas was spent at Ville-Sur-Ancre.

On January 7th we relieved the Guards at Sailly-Saillisel.

Sickness had sadly depleted the officers of ' D ' company ; only McKimm and I were fit enough to go into the line.

In the afternoon I started off at the head of the company, the sergeant-major bringing up the rear ; McKimm had gone forward to take over.

Marching along the road on the plateau we passed the huge army ammunition dump which was entirely destroyed a few days later by a bomb dropped by an enemy plane. It was unapproachable for days after.

We passed a battalion of the Guards on the way out of the line. They were in a very sorry state, having been on duty in the line for weeks.

Bearing to the right after Boilleux Wood we at last arrived in a sunken road, where we were ordered to wait until darkness fell ; there were dugouts here for shelter, so we were able to give the men a meal before we actually marched up the line.

At the end of this road there was a single tree, which in some miraculous way had escaped. Needless to say, this place

was christened ' Lone Tree,' and formed the chorus of a song.
Here it is :—

> Lone tree to Saillisel church
>   All on a winter's day,
> Up we got on the duckboards
>   And started right away.
> And when we got to the end of the boards
>   He said, " Won't you stop for a drink ? "
> But I said " they're shelling the chateau
>   So I don't think."

This was sung to Gertie Millar's famous tune, " Chalk Farm
to Camberwell Green," and was composed by our divisional
concert party, the ' Verey Lights.'

I led the company on to the duckboards at 8 p.m. No
sooner had I done so than the enemy opened up with a battery
of field guns, the shells falling in salvos on either side of us ;
it was alarming. I did not know whether to stop or go on.
I then remembered my brother's excellent advice : "Always
keep on the move," he told me, " if you stop you will lose
half the company from men falling out." I hesitated for a
second or so, till I heard a voice from the darkness say :
"—— officer's got the wind up." This decided me.

I went on, the company trailing behind me. I was walking
faster to get out of the shell fire ; if I had been alone I should
have run. Shouts of " go slow " from behind reminded me
of the company struggling along in the rear.

At the church McKimm was waiting to lead the company
into our positions ; as soon as the relief was complete we
retired to our headquarters to discuss hours of duty and so
forth.

McKimm decided to take night duty ; I was to relieve him
before dawn. I therefore took off my long thigh boots so that
they could be dried while I slept.

The next day it froze hard, which was an excellent thing,
as it made movement so much easier. The snow which followed
made visibility good ; snipers became a nuisance, it was
dangerous to walk about on the top.

Early one morning I was late in visiting one detached post.
The sergeant in charge kept me yarning ; I suddenly discovered

it was almost too light to get back with safety. However, I made up my mind to go, as I had no intention of staying in the post all day.

I jumped out of the trench to run to the trees; a bullet whistled past me; I lay down. After a pause I crawled on a few yards—'phut'—another, this time much too close to be pleasant. I did not know quite what to do. I saw two dead Germans a few yards in front. Dragging myself along the ground I lay behind them; they had been there a long time. I crawled on a little way—'phut'—another bullet. I lay still, my face to the ground. They might think I was dead. I waited ten minutes. This time I got up and ran as fast as I could to a trench I could see about thirty yards away. I fell into this panting for breath. No more shots so far. Dragging myself along the trench, there were two more corpses; I scrambled over them. Ugh! 'Phut'—just past my ears— this was too much. I got up and ran to the trees, dodging the shots, throwing myself into the trench near company headquarters. Safety once more.

The days passed quickly.

One lovely morning I was in an isolated post with six men, the sentry was looking over the top. Suddenly he exclaimed, " Sir, there's a Bosche carrying a bucket."

This roused us to immediate action.

" Lend me your rifle," I cried. " What's the range ? "

" Between 500 and 600," replied the corporal.

I took careful aim and pulled the trigger. The man with the bucket took no notice. Once again I took careful aim, putting the sight to 600; he leapt into the air, dropped his bucket, and ran for his life, disappearing from view. This little episode amused the men, and each morning they waited for him to appear.

McKimm and I did nine tours of duty in the line at this period. Finally we were relieved at the end of January. After a period of rest at Heilly we returned to our camp at Carnoy once more.

Soon afterwards we took over part of the line opposite Le Transloy.

CHAPTER V.

PURSUIT.

ON the night of March 16–17 McKimm and I sat in our dugout talking of nothing in particular.

A man entered.

" What is it ? " called out McKimm.

" The burial party is ready, Sir," he replied.

We both stumbled up the dark steps trying to get our eyes accustomed to the darkness.

A shadowy figure in the trench outside saluted.

" Is the padre there ? " McKimm asked the man.

" Yes, Sir ! He is waiting for you to come before he reads the service."

A few yards behind the trench we found the padre, standing by the grave of the unlucky man who had found a sniper's bullet.

We could just see the other two men who had dug the grave.

As we gathered round the grave the padre began the burial service.

The night was quiet ; occasional star shells from the German lines lit up our faces ; a spent bullet whistled by ; the war seemed to have stopped while we buried the poor chap.

The service went on.

Without warning it came, then another and another— 5.9's exploded with a crash and a roar within a few yards ; we hurriedly ducked—another shell was coming—much closer —it would drop almost on to us. The noise of its approach increased to a shriek ; we fell flat ; one man fell into the grave itself. A terrific explosion. Debris and earth fell all around us. As the smoke blew away we were relieved to see our party was intact.

Hurriedly the service was completed and the grave filled in before it started again. Placing a rude cross with his name to mark the place we left him.

A message was awaiting attention on our return.

" You will send out a strong patrol under an officer before dawn to reconnoitre enemy trenches. Report results immediately patrol returns," McKimm read out.

Turning to me he remarked :

" You had better take this patrol. You will have to make quite sure if the enemy are still there. Don't lose any men, as it is not intended to be a fighting patrol."

I left the dugout to make the necessary arrangements, and also to have another look at the lie of the land.

Le Transloy, or what remained of it, was about half a mile to our right, while the village of Rocquiny was about a mile in front. The ground beyond this village was undulating, so we could not see very far.

I gazed into the night trying to see what was happening, but it was too dark.

Surely the enemy were very quiet ? Much less active than usual. Their guns were now quite silent ; no star shells rose from their lines.

My patrol was to start at 4 a.m. ; there was time for a cup of tea with a tot of rum before starting.

" It is unusually quiet," I told McKimm, " not a star shell or anything."

" Funny," he replied. " I wonder if this rumour is true that they are going back."

" We shall soon know," I said. " It is time for me to be off."

I scrambled up the steps to find the sergeant ready.

" All present and correct, Sir," he said.

" Pass the word round to start and that men must keep in touch with each other. We shall cross to No Man's Land in groups of three, with an interval between each group. If they fire on us retire at once."

Scrambling out of the trench we found it difficult to get through our wire in the dark. This accomplished we moved forward in silence. Occasionally a man tripped up with a clatter of equipment ; we could now faintly see their wire, expecting a star shell to reveal our presence any minute. Nothing happened. We cautiously picked our way through the wire, cutting it with nippers in places. It was now evident that the front trench was unoccupied.

We soon found that the trench was empty. The rubbish of months of occupation lay about, the place smelt foul. The support line with some dugouts was deserted.

I decided to go back with the momentous news. It was getting light as we returned over the top. As we approached our line our men shouted that the German trenches were empty.

McKimm came along to see me.

" Is it true ? " he cried.

" Not a doubt about it," I said. " They went back last night. Those shells last night were a few they couldn't bother to take away."

The news was flashed over the telephone lines. Soon orders came through for us to advance as far as Rocquiny.

What a peaceful attack. Not a shot or a shell on this lovely spring morning as we walked across the old enemy front line. We could hardly believe it to be true. There must be a catch somewhere. We approached Rocquiny with caution, to find it unoccupied.

Here we halted to await orders. Looking back we could see our old lines which we had occupied for months from the enemy's point of view—Les Boeufs, Morval, Sailly Saillisel.

All our guns were silent. The war might have been over.

Open warfare. Not one of us had had any previous experience. We, who for months had done nothing but dig and burrow like moles, were now to experience something entirely different.

While we ate our rations a shout went up.

" The cavalry are here ! "

Sure enough a squadron of yeomanry passed by at the trot. Of course we gave them a hearty cheer. We watched them with great interest as they spread out into small patrols to reconnoitre ahead of us. One party dismounted at the base of a small hill, leaving men to hold the horses ; guns fired in the distance, their shells falling not far from the horses. The yeomen hurriedly mounted and retired. We roared with laughter.

We camped in the open that night, with sentries out in advance posts.

The next day we were ordered forward. Behind us we left a scene of great activity, as roads had to be made over the shell-scarred battlefields of the Somme. The guns were moving from the gun pits they had occupied for months ; the whole of the routine was altered by this enemy move ; they had retired in perfect order to the long-prepared Hindenburg Line.

They left nothing behind them. They had destroyed every house, and had even cut down the trees in the orchards.

Soon it was discovered to our cost that they had set clever " booby traps " for us. Steel helmets were left in deserted buildings which, when touched, sprung a mine, destroying the would-be souvenir hunter.

At Bus they left one house almost intact ; this was of course occupied as the mess of one of our battalions. They had not been there very long when the whole building blew up, with ghastly results for the occupants.

Orders were given that buildings were to be avoided in future.

While we were in Bus I was most comfortable in a pig sty, which I occupied after a minute examination.

Our advance at this time was covered by one field gun, which they had managed to extricate from the mud ; this was a change from the massed artillery we had been accustomed to.

For days we slowly advanced until finally our battalion came to a halt near the Canal du Nord.

Our company was quartered in a sunken road which led down to the canal bank, and on the other side the Australians held the line.

We were now only about two miles from the Hindenburg Line.

I was on duty one lovely spring afternoon in this road, lying on the bank of the canal reading a book, when a shout from the other side startled me.

" Say," called a man—an Australian soldier—" where does this path lead to ? "

" To Havrincourt Wood," I replied.

" I'm going to have a look at it," he said.

" Stop," I shouted.   " There is a Bosche machine gun post
in the corner ; don't be a fool."

The man had no equipment, just a rifle and a tin hat.

" I shall be all right," he laughed.   " I don't suppose the
Bosche are there."

It was nothing to do with us if he committed suicide.

We watched his progress with much interest.

Having lit a cigarette and slung his rifle over his shoulder
he strolled off down the canal bank whistling.   We could see
him stop opposite the end of the wood and look over to our side.
He then calmly proceeded to take his coat and boots off and
swam to the other side.   A series of splashes made it evident
that he was throwing the machine gun post into the canal.
He swam back and put on his clothes.   As he strolled up on
his return he shouted to us :

" I chucked all their —— goods into the canal.   They
won't half be wild when they come back to-night.   So long."

Off he went as if he had been for a walk in the park.

A night or two later we were ordered to advance by night
to the edge of Havrincourt Wood.

All went well until one of our advance patrols saw some
men approaching.   Luckily I was sent for just in time to stop
them killing some of our own men.

We then dug a line of posts in front of the wood ready for
the dawn, as we thought the wood would be occupied.

CHAPTER VI.

THE DAYLIGHT PATROL.

AT the first sign of dawn we redoubled our efforts to deepen the shallow holes which we had dug that night. We knew that the full light of day would instantly reveal our positions to the enemy.

As it became lighter we could see our ragged line of posts extending on either side for some way. We were on a gentle downhill slope leading to the edge of Havrincourt Wood, the trees of which covered the slope on the opposite side of the valley for about half a mile.

Everyone was in position awaiting the first signs of activity from the enemy invisible in the wood. The situation was tense as minute followed minute.

The sun gained power quickly dispersing the early morning mist, gradually revealing the various details of the landscape in front of us.

We saw that the trees had been felled as they stood ; they had been allowed to fall in all directions, with their branches still growing from the trunks, green with the fresh foliage of spring, unwithered as yet. Birds were singing. No signs of warfare here.

The sun rose behind the wood ; shadows flew before us. Bathed in warmth we grew hungry.

Men moved from their cramped positions to stretch their limbs ; the tension subsided, the wood before us was unoccupied.

Blue smoke from the small fires of our pickets rose straight up from the windless air. There was a delicious smell of frying bacon.

The day's work would soon begin in earnest, as our line had to be consolidated and my report of the night's operations despatched by runner to battalion headquarters. We were not to remain long in peace.

A runner arrived about 9 a.m. ordering me to send an officer's patrol to reconnoitre the wood. The message stated that information was required about the enemy line of defence in the wood, and also a report on the state of the bridges over the Canal du Nord. The message emphasised that the patrol must get in touch with the enemy and give specific information as to their whereabouts and numbers.

This was a pretty tough proposition which needed some nerve and experience, so I chose an officer who had been out a long time, and on whom I felt I could rely.

He started off at 11 o'clock, but I was amazed to see him walking at the head of six men who were following in a string behind him. This was bound to attract attention if the enemy were holding the wood—not the way to carry out the job at all. It was obvious that he had not the remotest idea of the proper way to do it. However, it was too late to stop him. Soon the officer and his patrol were lost to sight in the wood.

The morning passed peacefully with no sign of activity from the enemy. I was thankful that so far we had heard no firing from the direction the patrol had taken ; I waited anxiously for their return, it was now 12-30 p.m.

At 1 p.m. the officer could be seen emerging from the wood, still at the head of his six men. I breathed a sigh of relief.

Rather dubiously I sent his written report to battalion headquarters by runner. It was far from clear. There was no concise information which could be acted upon by those higher up. It was too vague.

Later I was sitting in our so-called company headquarters when the telephone buzzed.

" The adjutant to speak to you, Sir," the signaller said.

" Hullo, is that you, Tim ? "

" Yes. Can you come to battalion headquarters right away ? "

" Of course. What's wrong ? "

" Oh, that report is no good, and the Colonel wants to see you."

" Is he peeved ? "

" Yes, a bit. I am afraid you will have to do it, old man ! "

" Hell ! Why can't he make him do it again ? "

" Don't know. He seems to think you will have to do it yourself and make a proper job of it. Sorry, old man ! It's not my fault, you know ; come as soon as you can."

There was nothing else for it but to go to see the Colonel at once, and so off I went feeling very sore. Why on earth should I have to do the job ? A patrol in broad daylight, too. By this time the enemy would probably be ready and waiting.

Arriving at battalion headquarters I went at once to see the Colonel, who received me immediately.

" I suppose you have read this ? " he said, handing me the report. " Quite useless. You will have to go yourself and do it again. I'm of course sorry you should have to go, but it was your business to see that an officer was sent who was capable of doing the job. I want the report here by 6 p.m. at the latest."

Feeling very annoyed I returned, pondering on the best way to organise the patrol, and deciding whom I should take with me.

As soon as I arrived at company headquarters I sent for the sergeant-major—a really old hand—a small rugged man with a big moustache and the heart of a lion.

He came in and saluted.

' Sergeant-major," I said, " get hold of six good men. We have to take a patrol into the wood, which will take an hour or so. You will send out ahead two scouts, the second man fifty yards behind, you and I fifty yards behind him. The others will be in pairs acting as flank guards about one hundred yards on each side of us.

" Very good, Sir," he replied.

" We start in half an hour, taking as little as possible ; just rifles and a bandolier to each man."

We started from company headquarters and soon reached the wood, where we found our progress was very slow, owing to the fallen trees.

Quickly losing sight of our line behind us we proceeded slowly and cautiously for about half a mile into the wood, when the advance scout sent back a message reporting that he could see in front of him a system of trenches guarded by barbed wire.

Ordering our men to be ready to support us I went forward with the sergeant-major to investigate.

We found that the trees had been cleared to give a field of fire in front of the wire, and that there was a gap through which we could reach the trench. Without a sound we crawled down the path through the wire, ready for anything. We came to the trench itself.

Looking over the top we found it empty, but a little to our right we saw what was obviously the entrance to a dugout, as it had a blanket covering the door.

" Sir," whispered the sergeant-major, " if you will be ready with your revolver I will pull the blanket back with the point of my bayonet ; I expect the Bosche are asleep."

I got ready, thrilled to the marrow.

" Ready, Sir ! " he exclaimed, wrenching away the blanket.

There was no one inside.

We found a scrupulously kept small room, six rifles neatly stacked against the wall in a rack, a pile of bombs, tins of water, cases of ammunition, piles of blankets, etc.

We heaved them all out into the bushes. The Germans would be annoyed when they came back that night.

We proceeded to explore the trench system for about two hundred yards on either side. I made a rough sketch giving its position in the wood, and in my report stated that cavalry could not possibly circumvent it.

We then ordered our scouts forward, proceeding onwards in the same formation for about another half mile. Once again the scouts ahead halted and we went forward to see for ourselves what was the matter.

The leading scout crept back on all fours.

" Bosches are just ahead in the village, Sir. Hundreds of them, not more than half a mile in front," he muttered hoarsely.

" Right," I whispered. " You all stay where you are and make sure you are not seen. I am going forward to see for myself."

I crept forward to the place the man had come from, and a most interesting scene met my eyes.

I could see the village of Havrincourt, quite undamaged by shell fire, about half a mile away, nestling in a hollow below me. On the left was the Canal du Nord, with its bridges destroyed, and on the opposite slope the trenches of the Hindenburg line.

I sat down on a fallen tree to draw a rough map of the ground I could see, putting in the broken bridges, etc. I also wrote a report.

All this time I could see the German soldiers walking about the village on their various jobs or lying on the grass in the sun. The sergeant-major lay besides me smoking his pipe.

Suddenly, to my utter amazement, an observation balloon started to rise under my very nose it seemed ; it must have been concealed in a hollow where I could not see it. Slowly it rose to about two hundred feet, becoming stationary almost above us. We could see the two men in it looking down with field glasses.

" Keep quite still, Sir," whispered the sergeant-major. " They may not see us."

Just then they did see us. We could see the officer with the glasses pointing down towards us ; he reached for his telephone ; we could imagine him reporting our presence. What was to be done ?

" We must get back at once ! " I exclaimed to the sergeant-major. " Tell the men to go back in the same formation."

Four guns spoke in the distance. Four shells shrieked over to fall in the wood, a good three hundred yards away.

" They have not seen us, Sir," said the sergeant-major.

Four more shrieks and four more shells fell one hundred yards short of us.

" They have spotted us," he shouted.

He shouted to the men to hurry. We ran as best we could, stumbling over the branches. Four more shells burst with a ' crump ' over us, but high up ; balls of black smoke blew away in the wind. I could imagine the Bosche officer in the balloon shouting guttural directions to the batteries through the telephone.

Four more shells arrived. This time too close for comfort, just over our heads. They had got the range ; rapid fire commenced ; we had hardly time to drop when we heard the shriek of the shells coming. They were firing with high velocity guns and firing them as quickly as they could load.

A salvo dropped right in the middle of us, bursting right at the height of our heads. Chips whistled through the foliage ; clouds of black smoke choked us. I was getting panicky, so were the men ; as soon as we moved another salvo arrived. We were all wounded, none of us seriously. My hand was bleeding pretty badly.

Something had to be done, and that quickly, or we should have the Huns from the village after us.

I got up and shouted : " Every man run fifty yards to the right and then double back towards home, every man for himself."

The sergeant-major and I ran like hares, dropping behind trees each time we heard the guns fire. They lost the range a bit ; we were scattered and not so easy for the people in the balloon to see.

Back through the wood we ran, panting for breath, our clothing torn, faces blackened. We were a dishevelled party when we once again emerged from the wood to find all our troops standing up wondering what all the shooting was about. They thought that a miniature war had started.

After resting for a bit I handed in my report and the Colonel was most amused at my account of our adventures. He seemed to think it a huge joke. I didn't see anything funny about it myself.

The main thing was that he was pleased with the report.

CHAPTER VII.

THE CAPTURE OF TRESCAULT.

A FEW days later we were sitting under trees in the north side of the wood, as our short rest at Royaulcourt was over. We were to take over the front line that night.

An orderly handed a message to McKimm.

" Here's a message from battalion headquarters telling me to send out an officer to reconnoitre Trescault from the wood. It suggests you," laughed McKimm.

" Well, I'm damned ! Let someone else go ! " I replied.

" You will have to go. You made your reputation on the last one," he jeered.

" Right ho ! Will after lunch do ? " I asked, as I rose to go.

" Yes, but you had better go to orderly room to find out what they want to know," he shouted after me.

Smith got up to follow me.

" Can I come with you ? " he asked.

" Whatever for ? " I replied. I could not think of anyone wanting to go on such a job.

" I would like to come with you if you don't mind," he said.

" I don't mind, as long as you promise to be good and not take any risks, and also do what I tell you," I replied.

He laughed and agreed.

Smith was a small man, not much to look at, but he had the pluck of a lion ; he was not a safe person to go about with, he took too many risks.

They explained to me at battalion headquarters that there was to be an attack on Trescault in a day or two by our brigade, covered by quite a formidable barrage of two batteries. The powers that be wanted to know in what strength it was occupied, and as much else as they could find out about it.

I decided to start at 2-30 p.m. with Whittingham, telling Smith to take his orderly with him. The fewer we were the better, I thought.

It was a lovely sunny afternoon when we started away through the wood, which was not felled hereabouts. Soon we reached the outposts, which were held by a brigade who did not know us. Luckily we held passes, otherwise they would not have allowed us to pass through their lines. The officer in charge was suspicious and officious.

" Do you think we are Bosche spies, or what ? " asked Smith.

" You might be anything as far as I know. What the devil do you want to come through our lines for ? " he exclaimed.

" Look here, my lad," I replied, " you keep quite calm and read this."

" That's all right," he said, after reading the pass.

We left the disagreeable little beast and soon his post was out of sight. We proceeded with caution now, as we were not sure if the wood was occupied or not. We had walked about half a mile beyond the post when we saw, about one hundred yards away, the edge of the wood, with freshly dug earth, indicating a trench line.

We decided to advance together, with Whittingham and Smith's orderly on our flanks, with their rifles at the ready in case anything happened.

The trench system was unoccupied, but we could easily see from there down into the village about a quarter of a mile away.

The enemy were quite numerous, walking about and standing talking in groups. A thin line of wire extended as far as we could see round the village, but there appeared to be no system of trenches.

Having noted all particulars we quickly departed, as we came, and eventually reported to battalion headquarters the result of the patrol.

Preparations were then pushed forward for the attack two days afterwards.

The night before the attack was to take place Trescault was captured by one officer and six men.

A young officer of one of the brigades was in charge of a post in the sunken road north of the village. Each night he had been annoyed by a German machine gun, which fired down the road at unexpected moments, making movement for himself and his men unsafe.

This officer, aged twenty years, decided on that particular night that he and his men would shift that machine gun.

At the time arranged for ' Zero ' they crept down the edges of the road very quietly. In the dark they could not be seen. When they were within bombing range each man withdrew with his teeth the pin of his Mills bomb, and when the officer gave the word they all threw them at the machine gun, or where they thought it was.

Six explosions—shouts—sounds of running feet—silence.

They rose to their feet. Gingerly advancing toward the machine gun emplacement they arrived to find it deserted.

They quietly went on down the road, eventually reaching the edge of the village. Hearing voices they entered the house nearest to them ; with a clatter two men bolted by the back door.

The officer and his six men searched the house, finding no one, but from the first floor they saw some of the enemy. They opened fire from the window, causing the Germans to bolt.

At this point the officer decided to send a message to his Colonel.

" Have entered village. Enemy retiring. Please send to reinforce me."

He and his party then proceeded to walk up the street until they came to another house which overlooked the Square or Market Place. From the first floor they saw the Germans leaving at the other end.

Again they opened fire to hasten their retreat.

Shortly afterwards they ventured further on to find the village empty.

A message was sent back.

" Have captured village."

As a result the village was occupied by our troops without a single casualty. The officer got the D.S.O., which he earned by showing initiative and pluck.*

In front of Havrincourt we proceeded to dig in, and for a few weeks very little of interest happened.

---

* The name of this Officer was Lieutenant A. D. Thornton-Smith, who was afterwards killed at the Battle of Langemarck.

Eventually we moved into the line near Bapaume, where it was quiet. Our leisure moments, when out of the line, were enlivened by a huge 13″ naval gun, which fired from Lille. When this gun was shelling our vicinity we vacated the spot hurriedly.

In June we were taken out of the line for battle practice.

CHAPTER VIII.

REST AND INTENSIVE TRAINING.
JULY, 1917.

FOR some weeks we led a quiet life in billets at Domart, a village not far from Amiens.

Battalion headquarters were at this time in the same village, so for the first time all the officers of the battalion messed together.

We were ordered to be inoculated against typhoid again. In consequence I retired to bed for three days, feeling very sick with a high temperature.

Intensive training was the order of the day; musketry, bombing, bayonet fighting and training in " The platoon in the attack."

It was obvious to all of us that we were being " fattened up " for something pretty big. Already rumours of the impending offensive near Ypres had reached us. These did not prevent us from making the most of the ' rest ' period, for Amiens was quite near enough to enable us to spend many cheery evenings at the Hotel Universe and other places of amusement.

As battalion intelligence and sniping officer I had plenty of work to do.

Headquarters had issued a new order for the training of " Snipers for use in the attack." Therefore the two best shots in each company were seconded from all duties for training.

Their job, when the objectives were reached, was to protect our men from enemy snipers when digging in, to make a particular mark of enemy machine gun posts, and during a counter attack to pick out German officers.

They were trained to work together in pairs, one man firing at a time, while his mate found the target and reckoned the range.

Excellent telescopic sights and field glasses were supplied.

The men were very keen, and in the attack which followed they helped very considerably to keep down casualties.

Our time table at this time was as follows :

The men had breakfast at 7 a.m. ; afterwards the officers inspected equipment and rifles ready for company parade at 9 a.m. From 9 a.m. there was rifle drill and company drill until 10 a.m., when companies dismissed for Lewis gun practice, bayonet fighting, bombing and gas drill.

After lunch the men did pretty well what they liked, except when we were practising for the attack.

A few days before we moved nearer the front we were inspected by the divisional commander in the morning, and one platoon gave a very realistic display of " The platoon in the attack " in the afternoon.

We moved to Proven, near Poperinghe, on or about July 21st, arriving in our hutment camp in the evening. This camp was comfortable, but we suffered from air raids nearly every night. The planes were probably after a huge naval gun, which fired from the railway not far away.

There was an excellent officers' club in Poperinghe, but beyond this we found the country and the people very depressing. In consequence we were not really sorry when the time came for us to move on.

On the last night the Colonel invited the officers of a French battalion (the Chasseurs Alpins) to dine with us. They were a cheery crowd. Consequently we spent a very enjoyable evening. Few of us could speak any French, and they could not speak English. However, under the influence of an excellent dinner, and still more excellent champagne, we managed to converse quite a lot.

On August 3rd all officers made a reconnaissance of the line.

Starting from Proven, at 9 a.m., in London buses, we passed through Poperinghe into flat depressing country ; the roads, lined with poplars, were very bad. The whole country was very wet, rather resembling our Fen district.

Very few signs of the war were in evidence until we arrived at Elverdinghe. The church was badly knocked about, but although the houses were damaged here and there by shell fire, they were still fit to act as billets for troops.

The road traffic in both directions was very heavy, but was kept under control by military police.

Arriving near the canal bank we were told to walk along

the bank until we reached Essex Farm, where we should find guides. Essex Farm was not a farm, but a large casualty clearing station on the canal bank. Here a good bridge had been built over the canal. Crossing this we met our guides, who were to lead us to brigade headquarters.

We were dressed in full battle equipment, with gas masks. I had taken sandwiches and a flask as well.

We passed through a gap cut in the embankment on to the open country, which sloped gradually up to Pilkem Ridge, a mile or so in front. This was captured in the attack on July 31st.

It was a most desolate scene—not a building remained; only the stumps of shell-torn trees gave any indication of the spinneys which must have dotted the landscape.

Shell holes, great and small, full of water, covered the whole area, making movement for man or beast almost impossible without artificial means.

Duckboard tracks were laid the whole way to brigade headquarters, while roads made of sleepers led to the battery positions.

It was a most dreary prospect, made worse by the faint smell of gas and decomposing corpses, human and otherwise.

We were very interested in the old front line which our troops had held like grim death since the early days of the war.

These men had constructed in No Man's Land a steel tree copied from a broken-down willow. It was impossible to tell that it was faked from fifty yards. It was used to conceal a sniper.

Passing along the rickety duckboard track, in single file, we came upon a mule in a shell hole, up to its neck in water. We left the artillerymen still trying to get it out, after watching their efforts for some time ; their language was picturesque.

Brigade headquarters were at Stray Farm, or, I should say, they were in the cellars of Stray Farm, as nothing but a heap of rubbish remained of the farm itself.

We were told that from the top of Pilkem Ridge we should be able to see the ground sloping down to the Steenbeek Brook, where our present front line lay, and beyond the brook the ground would slope gradually up to the village of Langemarck, our objective in the forthcoming attack.

We left in pairs, so that we should not be too conspicuous when we appeared on the skyline. Picking our way cautiously between the shell holes, tripping over concealed lengths of barbed wire, slipping, stumbling, and incidentally, cursing, we at last reached the top of the ridge. Simultaneously many other couples appeared on the skyline on each side of us. For a minute or two we looked with interest at the view in front of us. We had barely time to discover on our half-left front the village of Langemarck when the enemy proceeded to put down a barrage all along the top of the ridge.

Screaming shells fell in front and behind us, bursting in the sodden ground ; they threw up masses of mud and water, soaking us. Dodging the shells as best we could, we ran down behind the ridge until we arrived in comparative safety. Here we sat down to wait until the shelling ceased.

After about half an hour we cautiously made another attempt to reach the top of the ridge. This time we actually crawled for the last part.

It was no good. The enemy was evidently on the look-out for his guns opened fire once again. One of our officers was hit, so the reconnaissance was abandoned for the day.

On or about August 10th we moved into bivouacs at Malakoff Farm, in the open fields, not far from the canal. The men slept in holes about 18″ deep, covered with their ground sheets. We were fortunate enough to find a disused gun pit.

The day before we left Proven a notice appeared in Orders that those who wished to attend a Communion Service should meet at the local place of amusement at 6-30 p.m.

As I walked to the entertainment hall I could not help recalling the last time I paid it a visit. On that night the concert party had excelled themselves, making the packed house roar with laughter.

I did not expect to find many others there on this occasion.

The room was full of silent men. Late arrivals crept quietly in to fall on their knees in prayer before sitting down on the rough benches.

The room had a stage at one end lit by two oil lamps. On this the padre was doing his best to rig up an altar with the materials at hand. A table cloth had been used to cover the packing cases of which it was constructed.

Oblique photograph taken from an aeroplane of the Battlefield of Langemarck before our bombardment.

Bread and wine had been obtained from the club.

The silence in the room was intense as the padre entered in his robes to commence the service. Outside the noise of passing transport and the distant sound of guns could be heard.

The padre started the service. His congregation murmured the responses.

I felt at peace ; away from the war and all the beastliness it entailed ; the others must have felt the same.

When the time came officers and men followed each other up to the improvised altar to receive the Sacrament.

As the last communicant left the altar we could hear the impatient crowd outside waiting to come in for the night's entertainment.

Silently and thoughtfully we dispersed to our various destinations.

Those who have lived to remember will never forget that service.

At this camp we were within range of the German guns, so gas sentries were posted each night.

The second in command, who was in charge of the battalion, decided to hold a church parade on the Sunday, although we protested vigorously, pointing out the danger of a daylight air raid or enemy shelling. However, as he insisted on the parade taking place the battalion was formed up at 11 a.m. in a hollow square and the padre began the service.

A quarter of an hour had elapsed when we heard the drone of many aeroplane engines in the distance. A large squadron of enemy planes were flying in our direction—six Gothas and about ten fighting planes not more than 1,500 feet high.

The observation balloon behind us was hauled down with great speed.

There was no time to dismiss the parade.

The Major gave the command for everyone to stay where they were ; the best thing he could have done. If we had started moving about they certainly would have seen us.

They flew over us in beautiful formation.

As soon as they had passed the battalion was ordered to dismiss and scatter. Anti-aircraft Lewis guns were ordered to be got ready for the return of the planes.

They dropped countless bombs on the artillery horse lines about a mile behind us, killing many horses.   It must have been a horrible sight.   Before they started to return we could see three of our planes flying very high preparing to dive into the middle of the enemy formation.

When the enemy planes turned, flying in the same formation as before, our three planes dived, scattering them in all directions.   The Gothas quickly reformed to fly back to their lines, leaving their fighting planes to deal with ours.

Although every machine gun within range was firing no damage was done until they arrived just beyond our battery positions.   One was then hit and fell in flames.

Spent bullets were falling all this time like rain.

On August 12th we received the orders for the attack on August 16th.

Another attempt was made to reconnoitre the line, but this had to be abandoned owing to intense shell fire, which caused one serious casualty.

The battalion would therefore have to attack over unknown ground and try to capture objectives none of us had seen.

Orders were given for large scale maps to be prepared showing every detail of the ground we were to cover.   Special attention had to be paid to prominent landmarks on the flanks of the ground we were to attack.

It was my duty to make these maps from aeroplane photographs supplied by Army headquarters.   These photographs I compared with maps we already possessed.   I still have the original objective map used by the 6th K.S.L.I.

At this time a message was received at battalion headquarters stating that battalion intelligence officers could obtain from Army direct (without referring to brigade, division or corps) any aeroplane photographs they wanted, either flat or oblique.   The message added that if these photographs were not in the possession of Army headquarters an aeroplane would obtain them without delay.

I decided to take advantage of this message, as I knew Colonel St. John, who was Military Secretary to the Army Commander, General Gough.

I telephoned him, whereupon he asked me to lunch at Army headquarters at Chateau Lovie.

With the help of Whittingham I made myself as presentable as possible for such a great occasion, departing from the camp by lorry, and after many changes of transport I eventually arrived at the chateau.

Colonel St. John made me feel at home, but I was a little alarmed at the prospect of lunching with so many officers of high rank.

Before lunch I was introduced to the Commander of the 5th Army, General Hubert Gough ; his chief of staff, General Neill Malcolm ; the chief of the artillery, General Uniacke ; General Sargent, General P. G. Grant, and Colonels Maurice, Arbuthnot and Colthurst.

General Gough wished to hear from me all about our preparations for the battle, and it was most interesting to hear from him that our division had one of the most important objectives.

After lunch I went across to the intelligence office with Colonel St. John. He then left me with the officer in charge, who showed me all the latest photographs of our particular objective. These I took away with me.

I explained to him that we had made several attempts to reconnoitre the line, but without success.

On my return to battalion headquarters I found the General Plan for the battle had arrived.

The attack was to be launched at dawn on the morning of August 16th by the 5th and 2nd armies, assisted by a French corps on the extreme left.

The 14th corps, commanded by General Cavan, was to attack with the 29th division on the left, under General de Lisle, and the 20th division, commanded by General Douglas Smith, on the right ; the Guards division was to be in reserve. The 11th division was to attack on our right, and it was part of my job to keep in touch with them.

The 20th division was ordered to attack with the 60th brigade on the right, and the 61st brigade on the left, leaving the 59th brigade in reserve.

The 60th brigade was to attack with the Oxford and Bucks Light Infantry, who were to form up on the enemy side of the Steenbeek Brook. Their job was to capture the first two objectives, which were called the ' blue ' and ' green ' lines.

The 6th K.S.L.I. on the right and the 12th K.R.C.C. on the left were ordered to form up on our side of the Steenbeek, two hundred yards behind the Oxfords.

Both battalions were ordered to wait on the blue line until the Oxfords had captured the green line. They were then to advance through them to capture the final objective, called the ' red ' line.

Up to the green line our battalion was ordered to advance in artillery formation. For the attack on the red line 'A' and ' C ' companies were to advance as in " The platoon in the attack."

' D ' company was to act as a " mopping up " company with all sections of platoons in line. It was their duty to see that none of the enemy were left behind the attacking companies.

' B ' company was to be in reserve with the Colonel.

The men were to carry their iron rations, one day's rations, water bottles full, 120 rounds of ammunition, and two Mills bombs ; every other man to carry a shovel and an entrenching tool, and the rifle grenade sections three grenades each.

Every man was ordered to wear his box respirator in the ' alert ' position.

The whole plan was carefully explained to the men by platoon officers on the 14th. My objective maps were issued to the companies, the boundaries, visible landmarks, and conspicuous objects were pointed out to all officers taking part.

It was impressed on all ranks that when the red line was reached it should not be passed, as otherwise we should suffer casualties from our artillery.

Artillery officers explained the working of the barrage to us.

The artillery covering the attack of the 20th division was as follows :

91st and 92nd, 121st and 122nd brigades of the Royal Field artillery, a total of one hundred and eight 18 pounders and 4.5 howitzers, and the 8th Heavy Artillery Group, con-

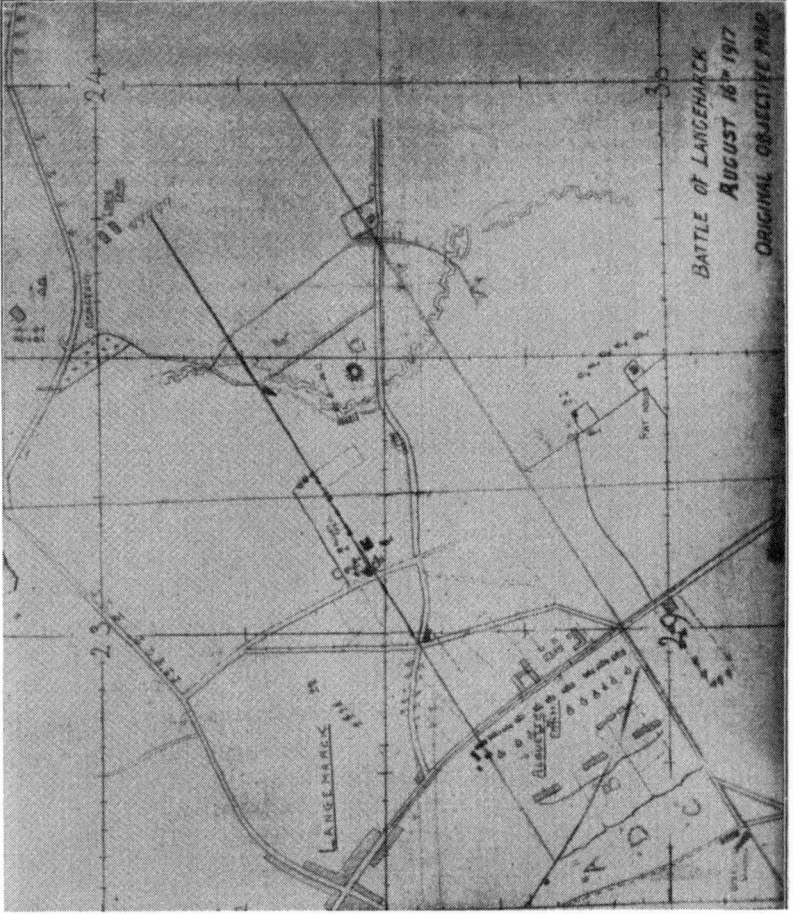

BATTLE of LANGEMARCK
AUGUST 16ᵀᴴ 1917

ORIGINAL OBJECTIVE MAP

LANGEMARCK

Direction of Attack →

Photograph of the Objective Map used by the 6th K.S.L.I. at the Battle of Langemarck.

sisting of twenty-four 6″ howitzers and twelve 8″ howitzers, a grand total of one hundred and forty-four guns.

The number of guns on the front of the whole attack was colossal.

Zero hour was fixed for 5-40 a.m., when the field guns and 4.5 howitzers would open barrage fire on the enemy front line ; that is to say, the guns would be fired as fast as the gunners could load them.

The other guns were to concentrate their fire on to the enemy batteries and back areas.

At Zero plus five minutes, that is to say, five minutes after Zero, the barrage was to lift and move forward one hundred yards at a time, while the troops advanced to their objective ; thirty minutes after Zero the barrage would stand in front of the blue line ; fifty minutes after Zero the barrage would move forward to the green line and stop there until one hour forty minutes after Zero, and then move forward to the red line, where it would remain until two hours after Zero.

This was a staggering programme. Thousands of tons of shells would be fired during those two hours.

The most elaborate arrangements were made to keep the troops in the line supplied with rations, ammunition, etc. No less than two hundred men, under four officers, were detailed for this job from the brigade in reserve.

The Royal Engineers were ordered to build duckboard bridges over the Steenbeek on the night of the 15th–16th, and next day to build more substantial bridges. This was a most hazardous task. Light railways were to be pushed forward as far as possible.

Lastly, the Machine Gun Corps were ordered to fire a barrage on to the enemy back areas over our heads. This was to start at Zero ; they were to use forty-eight guns per division for this purpose.

On ‘ Y ’ day—August 15th—we moved our quarters to dugouts in the canal bank.

Ammunition, bombs, rations, etc., were served out to the men in the morning, so that they should have the afternoon to themselves.

My snipers rejoined their companies to take their part on the morrow.

CHAPTER IX.

THE BATTLE OF LANGEMARCK.

IN the morning an orderly came to summon me to head-quarters.

I found the Colonel alone in his dugout ; before him was the map showing our objectives.

" Sit down," he said at once. "As you know, we have not seen the ground we are to form up on, let alone the ground we are supposed to capture."

" The thing is," he continued, " can you guide the battalion to the forming-up ground ? "

I had no time to reply ; he went on.

"Any way, I am absolutely relying on you to get them there somehow. I don't care how you do it. Company commanders have my instructions to detail whatever men you require for the job. When you get to the ground you must lay a tape showing the forming-up place of each company. I shall be there before Zero to see them for myself."

I told him I would do my best, and left, rather weighed down by so much responsibility.

The work I had done with photographs made me confident I should find the objects and landmarks where I expected them to be.

I met the company commanders, and after discussion it was decided to detail three men from each company as guides.

We were all to proceed to brigade headquarters at Stray Farm, where the first guides would meet their companies. These men would come with the others to the first rendezvous to learn its whereabouts, and then return to brigade headquarters.

The remainder would then go to the forming-up ground to help with the tape laying. When this was completed one guide for each company would return to the rendezvous and wait there till the first guide brought up his company. He would then lead the company to the forming-up ground, where the last guide would help place the company on the tapes.

This plan was carefully explained to the men and I arranged to meet them at 8-30 p.m.

After an excellent lunch we were at liberty to do what we liked. Most of us spent the time writing letters home. We began to realise, now there was a little time to think, that we were in for a big thing. How big we luckily did not know.

We had never taken part in an attack of such magnitude before.

I was not exactly frightened. I was strung up to a high pitch of excitement, and the thought of being killed did not seem to worry me much. My letters, which I saw afterwards, did not show signs of fear. I seemed to take it for granted I should get through safely.

Before mess that evening I found that Whittingham had everything in readiness for both of us, including a large flask of Justerini and Brooks brandy. I decided to take with me a very powerful electric signalling lamp, which was to prove useful. It was supposed to have a range of a mile in broad daylight.

The company commanders joined battalion headquarters' mess that night. I have forgotten the menu, but it was a good one. When the time came for me to leave they all rose to wish me luck.

" Have you got the brandy ? " I asked Whittingham.

" Yes, Sir ! Here it is," he replied, handing me my flask.

The guides were all present and correct.

" Follow me to Stray Farm—keep in pairs," I said. " There is no hurry. We do not start from there until 10-30 p.m."

Leaving the canal bank we followed the track, finding progress tricky in the darkness ; the duckboards were slippery and broken in places.

The guns in front of us were firing heavily, lighting up the night with their flashes. Shells screamed away into the distance ; as we moved nearer to these batteries the noise was deafening ; it was a scene of intense activity ; lines of mules and limbers were bringing up shells for the guns.

I was told afterwards that our heavies shelled the German batteries with gas all that night.

On arrival at Brigade headquarters I reported to General Butler, and stayed to have a few words with his staff, Major Hankey and Captain Hobart.

We started away on a previously arranged compass bearing. Keeping close together we stumbled along in the pitch dark, halting now and then for the others to keep up and to check our direction with my luminous compass. The going was very bad, our progress slow. Soon an object appeared ahead ; we found it to be a ruin of some sort with a few trees near it. After consultation with the others I decided to make this the first rendezvous. The position of brigade headquarters could be fixed by the light of the gun flashes.

Our eyes had now become more accustomed to the dark ; we could see a little way in front. Further on the German flares were lighting up the trees on the edge of the Steenbeek Brook.

The enemy started to drop whizz-bangs round us. Time to move on.

Sending the first three guides back to brigade headquarters we started again. The shelling increased ; 5.9's were now coming over, falling within fifty yards of us. We were compelled to drop for shelter frequently. The noise from our own guns now became deafening with the increased rate of fire ; the field guns opened fire, adding their share to the din ; we struggled on, tripping over wire, branches of trees, etc. We kept together ; during the whole journey we met no one. At last we could see the brook in front of us, about two hundred yards away. Continuously the enemy sent up flares ; they were nervous. I looked at my watch—it was past midnight.

The artillery fire behind us was now in full blast, their flashes lighting up the darkness all along the ridge behind us ; we had to shout to make ourselves heard.

The German artillery was now quiet.

We laid the lengths of wide tape for each company by the light of the gun flashes. They were easily seen. We could only guess at the proper positions, judging as best we could by the bend in the brook.

The three guides then returned to the intermediate rendezvous to wait for the battalion.

Our troops moving forward over shell-torn ground near Pilckem on August 16th, 1917. *(By courtesy of the Imperial War Museum. Copyright Reserved.)*

It was 1-30 a.m. when we completed the tape laying. We had a long wait before us with nothing to do except eat biscuits and drink mild brandy and water. We longed to smoke.

About 3-15 a.m. we could see a line of men moving in front of us. We hoped they were the Oxfords marching to their positions. For a moment we were not at all sure whether they were friends or foes . . . they disappeared. A few minutes later rockets of many colours rose from the German lines—S.O.S. Their artillery put down a barrage right on to us ; Whittingham and I lay in a shell hole quaking. Shells screamed over us, bursting all round us. What with the noise in front and behind it was pandemonium let loose.

It did not last long and soon ceased altogether.

To our amazement 'D' company, led by Kimpster, arrived from somewhere in front. They were led to their positions on the tape.

The battalion now started to arrive in real earnest ; we were kept busy sorting them out and answering questions.

The guides at the rendezvous had a dreadful time, I was told, all becoming casualties.

At about 4-30 a.m. the Colonel himself appeared, complete with staff and large silk handkerchief.

" Show me my battalion," he said.

After I had walked with him to see the companies we adjourned to a good-sized shell hole.

" Where did you leave Stanier, Sir ? " I asked.

" At battalion headquarters," he replied.

" Won't there be a spot of trouble over this, Sir ? " I asked tentatively.

" I expect so," he laughed. " I am not going back there now. I consider it my duty to stay with my battalion ; I can't help it if there is a row. I am used to them."

By this time our gun fire had decreased ; the field guns had ceased fire altogether, they were allowing the guns to cool.

At 5 a.m. the German artillery opened fire with a crash, a continuous line of flashes lit up the country in front of us. The rumble of their guns was one continuous roar ; shells of all calibres were crashing around us in hundreds, throwing up mud and water ; the air was thick with smoke ; debris and lumps of earth fell all around us. The sickly smell of burnt explosive was horrible ; the ground shook. It seemed impossible for anybody to survive this savage drum fire. A 5.9 burst within ten yards of the shell hole in which we lay, covering us with mud ; another fell closer still, burying us both. This was too much for me.

" Shall we go to another place, Sir ? " I shouted. " This is getting too hot."

" Find another hole if you know of a better one," he yelled back.

I thought better of it. We might as well go up together. I admit I was petrified with fear. They were coming down like hot cakes.

This went on until 5-30 a.m., ten minutes before Zero.

Suddenly it ceased. There seemed to be almost silence all along the front, both sides waiting. It was now much lighter. We could see the trees on the bank of the brook plainly now. Men began to move about, we could hear the clatter of equipment, the click of bayonets being fixed.

All fear left me. The horror of the past half-hour was forgotten. I was wildly excited.

Minute followed minute. Five more minutes to go ; the silence seemed to grow more intense.

We got ready to start ; one minute only now.

ZERO !

Every gun on the British front within a distance of twenty-five miles opened fire simultaneously. It is impossible to express in words the effect, it was stupendous. It was useless even to shout, the noise of the machine gun barrage drowned the noise of the massed artillery. It was shattering.

A wall of bursting shells fell in front over the brook, obliterating the landscape. We could see nothing beyond.

We rose to our feet shaking the dirt from our uniforms. Everyone lit a cigarette. Expecting to find half the battalion knocked out we were surprised to find very few casualties. Company commanders formed up their companies, the men carrying their rifles slung over their backs.

The Colonel waved us forward to cross the brook, which we found was bridged with duckboards.

There was no enemy shelling, their guns seemed to be completely silent.

I walked beside the Colonel, halting when we had crossed the brook.

The Oxfords were attacking in front of us. They were held up by a machine gun post in a concrete dugout called Au Bon Gite. They crept round it ; the occupants came out to surrender ; the Oxfords moved on. We followed on after them, halting on the blue line at 6-15 a.m.

We looked for our landmarks. There was the windmill on its side—that showed us our right boundary. However, to make sure the direction was checked by compass. Every object seemed to be much nearer than we expected.

All this time we were standing about waiting for something to happen. We could not see the Oxfords attacking the green line ; the situation became tense—where were the Oxfords ?

A long line of troops on either side of us stretched as far as we could see—masses of men. The barrage was standing in front of us ; soon it would lift for us to go forward.

At 6-30 there was still no sign of the Oxfords advancing to capture the green line. The situation was now critical. Someone had to do something.

German machine guns opened fire from a pill box no one had observed. The troops on our left were mown down like corn, their casualties were frightful. We lay down, the bullets whistling over our heads ; it looked as if the attack would be held up.

At 6-45 the barrage lifted, started to move forward, and was now quite a long way in front.

Colonel Wood made up his mind. Jumping to his feet, staff in hand, he waved his battalion forward with his bandanna handkerchief ; on each side the others followed his lead. The situation was saved.

We found afterwards that the Oxfords had been compelled to go round their objective and attack from the flanks, owing to the pill boxes.

I was a little in advance of the others ; in the excitement of the moment I had become separated from the Colonel. I came upon two Germans in a shell hole. Having a revolver

I pointed it at them.   They were terrified;   I felt rather
flattered till I found they had no rifles.   Not knowing quite
what to do I turned round to find the sergeant-major trying
to save my life ;   our men had seen them before I had and
were firing at them ; he was doing his best to prevent them
hitting me.

Shivering with fear they came out, hands in the air.   I had
captured two prisoners.

It was now 7 a.m.

Our advance was going well when a catastrophe of the worst
description happened.   The Colonel became stuck in the mud
and sank up to his waist.   I could not move him—he was a
man of ample proportions.   Assistance was promptly rushed
up and he was hauled out amidst loud applause ;   willing hands
scraped the mud from him.

At 7-15 we reached Allouette Farm, a very good German
concrete pill box which we had previously decided should be
our headquarters if we got so far.   The pill box was occupied
by a dead German officer, who had been there some time.   His
remains were speedily removed.

With help the place was soon made ship-shape.   It had
evidently been a dressing station as it contained a quantity of
field dressings which proved useful afterwards.

The entrance was facing the enemy, which was a nuisance,
especially as a concealed sniper fired at everyone who entered
or came out.   The Colonel ordered three men from ' B '
company to get him ; as soon as they started to surround him
he surrendered.

It was now time to commence our attack on the red line.
Our companies started at 7-35 to advance behind the barrage,
reaching their final objective with little opposition and very
few casualties at 7-45 a.m.

I was longing to try to signal to brigade with my lamp as
we had no men to act as runners.   Setting it up outside the
pill box I sent " We are here " in morse for ten minutes.
My knowledge of morse was small.   I never discovered whether
my messages were read ; the lamp, however, had been properly
christened.

No. 1 Message from Headquarters 6th K.S.L.I. (Code Word "Engage"). to Headquarters 60th Brigade (Code Word "Encore").

No. 5 Message.
Sent to Companies before first counter-attack. ("Enjoy" is Code Word for 12th K.R.R.C.)

The staff of battalion headquarters consisted of four—the Colonel and his orderly, Whittingham and myself. The Adjutant was still somewhere in the rear with all the battalion signallers and runners.

A message was sent to brigade headquarters by a company runner at 7-50 a.m., stating our positions and that the red line had been captured.

It was quiet in our vicinity so the Colonel and I went outside. Our men were about three hundred yards in front digging in ; in front of them in the distance we could see the Houlthoust Forest, and to the right of it the village of Poel-capelle, with a farm to the left, where we could see a German battery in action. In the rear our batteries were still firing heavily, but huge shells were falling amongst them, throwing up debris and mud to a great height. We did not envy the gunners; they had to continue working the guns whatever happened.

Our aeroplanes were very active and numerous ; all the enemy machines had been driven away.

We returned to the pill box to find a breakfast of eggs and bacon and coffee, cooked by Whittingham.

The Colonel was quiet ; he was tired.

" I wonder where Stanier is," he muttered. " I wish we could get hold of him."

" Where is battalion headquarters, Sir ? " I asked.

" Damned if I know," he replied.

There was silence for a short while.

" I shall probably get sent home for this," he said.

" I expect it will be all right, Sir, when they hear what happened on the blue line," I replied.

Whittingham came in to say I was wanted outside.

I found some of our men closely guarding two very dirty Germans. They both stood to attention ; they were bare-headed.

The tallest man addressed me.

" I must apologise, Sir, for my very dirty and unkempt appearance," he said in perfect English. " Your intense bombardment for the last three days has made shaving and washing impossible."

I was so astonished that I made no reply. I had not realised he was an officer.

The Colonel gave orders that he should be brought inside, so that he could cross-examine him on the dispositions of the enemy.

The German officer, standing strictly to attention, listened to him respectfully, but declined to answer any questions.

The General interviewed him at brigade headquarters with the same results. He was then sent down the line under escort with about fifty other prisoners, eventually arriving at Essex Farm, where they halted.

Our German officer calmly walked up to one of our medical officers :

" Excuse me, Sir," he said, " at your brigade headquarters I saw a large number of wounded. Would you like me to lead my men back there to act as stretcher bearers for you ? "

The medical officer was of course surprised, but thankfully accepted the offer of this gallant German officer.

All this time we were consolidating our positions and establishing contact with the people on our right.

Our aeroplanes went home to breakfast, leaving the air to the enemy, who arrived in swarms.

S.O.S. to our left was reported by the sentry at 9 a.m., the K.R.R.C. were being attacked on our left. Thin lines of the enemy could be seen from where we stood, advancing through a gap in our barrage, to form up on our side. Machine guns and rifles opened fire ; many of the enemy fell. They came on in open order, perfect discipline. They reached the K.R.R.C. positions. It looked as if they had captured them, as we could see our men being taken back as prisoners. The attack spread to the right, involving our left company. They were pressed hard ; things looked ugly.

An urgent message was sent to the Oxfords to send up a company to support our 'A' company. Messages were sent to the Machine Gun Company to rush two guns to help the K.R.R.C.

The rattle of rifle and machine gun fire was continuous. A trench mortar was sent to support the K.R.R's, doing great work. Our men on the left carried out a small counter attack,

No. 15 Message. To all Companies.

No. 6 Message.
To 6th Ox. and Bucks. L.I. (Code Word "Endure").

driving the enemy back. They retreated, taking some of our men with them ; the attack had failed.

At about 9-30 a.m. some of our signallers arrived with a supply of message pads. They reported that they had not seen Stanier.

The first message arrived by runner from brigade headquarters to congratulate the Colonel and the battalion on our victory. Not a word was said about his absence from battalion headquarters.

Nothing of any account happened for the next hour or so, but the enemy aeroplanes were very active. One came down in flames behind us. We claimed to have brought it down.

The German artillery woke up, their fire being directed on to all our positions by their planes ; none of ours seemed to be in the neighbourhood. We could see about two hundred of the enemy on our left. This information was flashed to brigade, who notified the artillery. The enemy disappeared in a cloud of smoke and bursting shells.

Urgent messages were sent to brigade for ammunition ; our left company had found they were short. At the moment we had no reserve supply to call upon.

At mid-day we were visited by two officers from Lord Cavan's corps. We gave them full details of our positions. They seemed to think we had done very well indeed ; we were of course surprised that they had come up so far to see for themselves ; it was a most unusual occurrence.

I went out to see them off returning to the pill box to find the Colonel fast asleep. I did not disturb him. I was so tired myself I could hardly keep awake. I sent a message to Stanier to ask him to hurry along himself with the battalion runners. I had been continuously on duty for sixteen hours.

Lunch was announced by Whittingham, who had managed to produce from somewhere excellent hot beans and bacon, with bread and butter. We had hardly finished when furious shelling was heard on our right, covering a counter-attack. From what we could see our men were falling back, leaving our flank exposed. The enemy were not numerous, so the Colonel sent up a platoon of ' B ' company to help. The enemy beat a hasty retreat ; it was a half-hearted affair. Our troops re-occupied their original positions.

At 4 p.m. I could plainly see great activity near Poelcapelle, in front of our lines. Battalion after battalion marched out of the village to the farm not far away, meanwhile the enemy artillery opened barrage fire all along our front line.

A counter-attack on a large scale was evidently intended.

The S.O.S. was sent up followed by a message to brigade headquarters giving the map reference of the enemy concentration. At this time there were very few signs of activity from our massed artillery in the rear.

For a minute or two nothing happened, then with a roar they opened fire. All the guns along our front were concentrated on one place, the shells shrieked and moaned over us ; immediately the farm in the distance was lost to view in smoke and flame. Rafters and masonry could be seen high in the air in the smoke, to fall again with a crash. The noise was stupendous.

Hurried messages came back from our front line. Some of our field guns were firing short, causing casualties to our troops ; brigade headquarters were informed by flag.

When the shelling ceased not a sign of the farm or the enemy could be seen.

The Colonel was asleep again. I was in such a state of exhaustion that I sent stupid messages to brigade headquarters. One said that the Colonel was exhausted and must be relieved ; another asked for the Adjutant to be sent to relieve me.

At 4-30 p.m. the most serious counter-attack of all developed on the brigade on our left, rapidly involving the K.R.R's. The enemy, as far as we could see for the smoke, had penetrated their line. We could see our troops retreating towards Langemarck. The K.R.R's showed signs of giving way. An urgent message was sent to 'A' company to hold on at all costs. Their left flank was reinforced by ' B ' company. Orders were sent to the Oxfords telling their ' B ' company to be ready to help at any time. The shelling was now very severe ; ammunition was running short ; things looked bad ; our flank on the left was exposed.

We could not see what was happening on our left for smoke. A message came from our left company asking for ammunition. We sent three boxes, all we had.

No. 16 Message.
To Brigade Headquarters giving map
reference of enemy concentration.

No. 20 Message. To 'A' Company.

We were entirely in the dark as to the position on our left.

The smoke cleared. We could see our men advancing. The position was evidently restored.

The Colonel at once went to sleep. I was in despair now— I had to keep awake somehow. I was worried about the Colonel ; he looked as if he was at his last gasp. I sent yet another message to brigade headquarters about him. Luckily they took no notice.

It was very quiet now in the pill box ; the Colonel was asleep, I smoked cigarette after cigarette. Whittingham brought me a strong cup of tea, to which I added brandy. I ate some biscuits. We had given up all hope of Stanier when he arrived with the battalion runners at 5-30 p.m.

I handed over my job to him. The Colonel woke up slightly refreshed ; he saw I was done up. He ordered me to report at once to the General and to explain his absence from battalion headquarters. He said he would not expect to see me again as we were to be relieved the next day.

Whittingham and I departed at once. It was quiet as we passed through the Oxfords and on to the brook, which was now well bridged by the Royal Engineers.

Arriving at brigade headquarters I was received by the General. I was so exhausted that I hardly knew what I was saying. I tried to explain the Colonel's absence from battalion headquarters ; he listened in silence. I went on to tell him how the Colonel had saved the situation on the blue line. He made no comment. He did not refer to my hysterical messages, thank goodness.

After I had finished all he said was :

" I think a good sleep would do you no harm."

I told him I had orders to go back to our base. He received this in silence. When I had finished all I had to say I fell asleep on the floor.

The Colonel did not get the sack, he got a bar to his D.S.O. instead.

We reached our base at Malakoff Farm in the early hours of the morning. The officers and men who were there crowded round me to learn all about the battle. I told them all I knew and then retired to bed.

The battalion lost five officers and about two hundred men in this battle.

The Colonel sent for me the next day. He informed me that he had recommended me for the M.C., also that he had sent my name forward for promotion. The latter was gazetted the next day.

I did not get my Military Cross then, as there were only three allotted to the battalion. These were awarded to the company commanders, who deserved them far more than I did.

We then marched back, depleted in numbers, to Proven, to refit and receive drafts for the next phase of the battle.

I went to England on leave.

Shell bursting near an 8″ Howitzer Battery, near Boesinghe, with gunners taking shelter
August 17th. 1917.
(By courtesy of Imperial War Museum. Copyright Reserved.)

CHAPTER X.

THE BATTLE OF THE RIDGE.

I RETURNED from leave in England on September 16th, 1917, knowing full well that I had to take part in another ' push.'

Tim had left for England, so I took over his job as Adjutant.

I found that our operation orders were complete for the attack on the 20th, and that the battalion was to move up to Malakoff Farm again on the morrow.

Most of us had now plenty of experience of battle on a big scale, therefore we had no illusions about the 20th ; in fact, the enthusiasm of a month ago was lacking.

On the night of September 19th the battalion marched up to Allouette Farm under better conditions than before, as the ground was now dry. The Colonel was sick, so Major Welsh was in command. He was a most conscientious officer, a great believer in seeing things for himself. He was quite fearless, and risked his life unnecessarily.

We departed for our headquarters before the battalion left, reaching Allouette Farm at midnight. We had some time to wait before the battalions arrived. The Major was getting anxious.

At about 1-30 a.m. a violent barrage was put down by the enemy. The first company chose this moment to arrive outside our concrete pill box.

A heavy shell fell just outside, blowing out our candles. Two men were literally blown inside the entrance. There was a scene of great confusion outside, many were killed and wounded ; there were shouts for stretcher bearers. The Major went out to do what he could to help. The pill box became a shambles, full of wounded men. We did our best, with our limited knowledge, to dress their wounds. One man was laid at my feet, badly hit. I examined him, to find to my horror that the whole of his thigh had been blown away. He was rapidly bleeding to death. No tourniquet was at hand ; even if there had been it would not have saved the poor chap. There was nothing to be done except to make his last moments as comfortable as possible. I gave him a cigarette and a pull from my flask ; fatal, of course, to give him alcohol. He said he was in no pain. He died peacefully in three minutes. We covered him over and laid him aside.

A sergeant came to me.

" There is something wrong with the back of my neck, Sir," he said, turning round.

I am not squeamish, but I felt sick for a moment. A piece of shell must have cut right through the fleshy part of the back of his neck, leaving the flesh hanging down over the collar of his coat. I clapped it back in its place, covered it with iodine and a wad of gauze, and tied it with a bandage round his throat and head. I told him he was now all right for Blighty, and pushed him out of the pill box, sending him down to the casualty clearing station. The medical officer told me afterwards that he could not have done the job better himself.

We soon cleared the walking cases, leaving Pooler to the last, who said he would wait. His clothing was torn to shreds, so we proceeded to strip him naked, at which he protested vigorously, shouting with pain. However, we had to do it, as he appeared to be wounded all over his body.

He had innumerable wounds. Little splinters of shells were sticking out of him, which we pulled out, dabbing the wounds with iodine ; others held him while we operated. Having removed the major portion of the splinters we dressed him again so that he could go to the casualty clearing station. He was back with us in three weeks full of beans.

There were no more cases, which was lucky, as we had run out of dressings.

The Major decided that this pill box was too unsafe, so we moved on to another about three hundred yards away on the left, called " Double Cottages."

We arrived there just before the attack was due to start, and I heartily wished we had stayed where we were. It was a disgusting little pill box, the entrance half facing the enemy. It seemed to be inhabited by about five million flies, and smelt horribly.

No rations had arrived, but luckily we found about six

boxes of *petit beurre* biscuits, twenty or thirty tins of water
and last, but not least, three jars of rum ; we survived for
the next three days on these rations.

I was a trifle tired by the events of the night, so lay down
in a bunk to rest for a bit. The bed was harder than usual,
and after a quarter of an hour I could stand the discomfort
no longer. I found, on investigation, I was lying on four
sandbags filled with candles.

I missed Whittingham. He had been sent to the other
pill box to fetch something. Where was he ? Going out with
one of the runners we found him staggering along. He had
been hit. We took him in, to find that he had quite a nasty
wound in his side, so we bound him up and sent him off down
the line. Thank heaven he was back with us in a fortnight.

The attack was not a success that morning ; only part of
our objectives were gained.

During the attack, and throughout the three days we were
in the line, I had to remain in the pill box. The shell fire was
terrible. I had never experienced anything like it before or
since.

Apparently the pill box we were using was in the centre
of their barrage line. Whizz-bangs and 4.2's fell in front,
5.9's to both sides and on to the top, and 8″ just over us. If
one of the latter had hit the pill box it would have collapsed ;
as it was some came so close that the whole thing rocked like
a ship in a heavy sea. About every five minutes, during an
intense bombardment, the pill box received a direct hit, the
blast blowing out candles and leaving us in darkness. No one
could come in or go out whilst this lasted ; it would have been
certain death. We lay or stood as far away from the entrance
as possible, waiting for the next direct hit, hoping that the
roof would hold out.

Meanwhile the five million flies buzzed around, settling on
our food, giving us no peace.

We lived on rum and water and *petit beurre* biscuits.

When things quietened down a little the Major insisted on
leaving us to visit the companies in the line. Several times
he was absent for hours, while important messages arrived
from brigade which had to be dealt with at once. I was
virtually in command of the battalion for long periods.

One night, when he was away, an urgent message came through that there was to be an attack by the battalion on our left. We were to give what assistance we could.

My friend Lloyd was commanding our left company.

I sent him a message telling him to assist as best he could when the attack took place. He sent back a cheery reply. I heard later he was killed.

Day after day, night after night, passed. I lost all sense of time.

Again and again we attacked, to meet with little success.

Counter-attacks, accompanied by intense barrage, were launched by the enemy with the same results. The battalion fought well, suffering severely. Deeds of great bravery were the order of the day.

The Major was hardly ever inside his headquarters. Messages came from brigade by runner. It was impossible to keep the telephone wires working, the breakages were too frequent.

Our runners were magnificent. I allowed them to go with the lightest possible equipment on their errands. They went in rushes, falling as a shell burst, getting up again, gaining a bit more ground each time, till they finally got to their destination.

At last the Adjutant of the Oxford and Bucks arrived. I was ' all in.' The battalion had been relieved. We were the last to go.

We left early in the morning. A thick mist obliterated the landmarks ; but for a few bursts of machine gun fire now and then everything was quiet.

I walked down a well-worn track, followed by the others. The ground was powdered to the fineness of salt by the shells. Limbs and parts of bodies turned up by the shell fire lay exposed.

A challenge came from our front. We had walked almost on to the top of a post held by three men.

" Where the hell do you chaps think you are going ? " they cried. " I suppose you know this is the front line ? "

We were going in the wrong direction and turned back swiftly to retrace our steps, to find ourselves once more at headquarters.

The mist was clearing. We hastened on our way out, this time in the right direction—Allouette Farm, down the broken duckboard track, past Au Bon Gite to the brook, and on to brigade headquarters.

Malakoff Farm again, and so to bed, tired out.

Our troubles were not yet ended.

That night we were shelled at midnight with gas. We had to rouse up the men and evacuate the camp until it died down.

A gas shell had dropped in a bivouac with horrible results.

Our nerves were badly shaken.

Next day we moved back once more to our old camp at Proven, to lick our wounds and refit.

CHAPTER XI.

The Train Journey.

THE camp was in a wood. They had built it there so that the prying eyes from above should not see it. Perhaps they had failed to see it—who knows? It did not seem like it to us.

Every night the shout of " lights out—air raid " sounded through the camp, spoiling our sleep, undoing all the good the so-called " rest behind the line " was supposed to be doing. One could stand that sort of thing for a time, but there were limits. Was I beginning to crack? I had made no mistake yet ; no one knew.

It was a quiet afternoon and the day's work was over. Tim Stanier and I sat in the orderly room talking of nothing in particular. We were bored. His mind kept returning to London, dinners at the Carlton, the Empire, and the girls he had met. Poor devil, he had only arrived back from leave a day or two ago. I let him go on yarning, there was nothing else to do.

My leave had long since passed from my mind—a dream of a month ago.

I felt a fatherly interest in Tim as he talked of his adventures in far-away London. He was so very young—more than eight years younger than I.

" I suppose we shall move out of this hole soon," he grumbled, and, after a pause :

" I heard a rumour to-day that they were going to send us to the Somme again. I wish they would. I'm fed up with this camp and the bombing. We are supposed to be safe here ; I don't think."

His last remark made me think a bit. . . . Did he also live in terror of these nightly raids?

I did not tell him that every night when " lights out—air raid " was shouted I crept from my tent unable to sleep, listening with a sickening feeling at the pit of my stomach for the well-known ' drone ' of the hostile plane, and, hearing it coming in our direction, proceeded to lie in a ditch while the infernal machine dropped its eggs all around me, dreading the next bomb.

The noise of the anti-aircraft machine guns added to my nightly terror. I could hear their spent bullets falling through the foliage like large drops of rain before a thunderstorm. I lay and shivered, hoping no one would find me, wondering how I should explain it if they did. It was funk, sheer unadulterated funk.

Steps approached ; the door opened to admit a signaller, who saluted and handed Tim a written message.

Tearing it open he exclaimed :

" Here we are—move to-morrow, entrain at Proven station at 5 p.m."

" Does it say where to ? " I asked.

" Not a word. I'll read it to you : ' The 6th K.S.L.I. will entrain at Proven at 5 p.m., October 7th. Details later.' "

I took my departure to tell the others. I also had to find Whittingham, as my valise would have to be packed ready to go with the heavy luggage on the morrow.

The next day we marched to Proven and commenced the usual job of allotting the troops to their ' compartments ' in cattle trucks marked " Hommes 40, Chevaux 8."

My job over I went along the train to choose the cleanest first-class carriage I could find, with as many sound windows as possible. I placed my case in a corner seat.

The train was due to leave in a few minutes. I was soon joined by Tim and two of the others. After a delay the train started with difficulty, all of us leaning out of the windows, cheering, singing and shouting ribald remarks to the railway transport officer. As the train left the station behind my only comment was, " I hope to goodness I never see Pop or Wipers again. Too much intense warfare for me. I want a quiet life for a bit."

" Same here," agreed Tim.

" And so say all of us," echoed the others.

" We seem to be proceeding at about four miles per hour," remarked Smith, who was leaning out of the window. " I suppose we spend the night here, don't we ? "

" What do you expect ?   A bedroom and bath ? " grunted Tim.

By this time it was dark, so I lit my candle, stuck it in its own grease on the window sill, and settled down to continue my novel about an officer who had met a marvellous girl in the South of France, who turned out to be a German spy.   I was just getting to the part where she was extracting important secrets from him in exchange for her embraces, so the conversation of the others no longer interested me.

I suppose two hours had passed when I suddenly realised the train had stopped.   Looking at my watch I found it was 9-30 p.m.

As the train had stopped we all got out.   It was not the Great Western Railway ; in France, whenever a train halted, we always got out to investigate and to talk to people, etc. There was no danger of the train suddenly departing without us.   There was always time to get in again when it started to move off.

We were standing on a fairly steep embankment ; a few lights from a town could be seen glimmering feebly in the distance.   It was a lovely night, with no wind ; a full moon was shining almost over our heads in a star-lit sky.   It was very quiet.   No longer could we hear the sounds of war or see the flicker of gun fire on the horizon.   It was superbly peaceful. We felt SAFE.

We went to the front of the train, because Tim wanted to know why we had stopped.   The French engine driver and fireman had descended to the ground, but we could not make head or tail of what they were saying.   I suppose it was something about signals.

" Listen ! What's that ? " whispered Tim, suddenly seizing my arm.

" I can't hear anything," I answered.

" You must be deaf. Can't you hear an aeroplane ? " he replied.

" You are right," I agreed. "And there's more than one. What is more, they don't sound like ours ; surely it cannot be the Huns as far back as this ? "

"Anyway," urged Tim, " whatever they are they are coming towards us. If they are Huns they can't help seeing the train ; they will give us hell if they spot us."

A man ran up ; we couldn't see who it was.

" The Huns are coming, Sir, three of them. I saw their marks."

" Don't panic," Tim replied. " I can't do anything if they are."

Just then we saw the French driver and stoker legging it for all they were worth down the line towards the town. Orders were being shouted : " Take cover in the ditch ; Hun air raid."

I was alone. Tim had left me ; the planes were almost on us, not very high ; the droning noise of their twin engines grew louder and louder. Suddenly we saw them in the moonlight.

" There they go," someone shouted.

I had seen them too, no need to tell me. I literally fell down the embankment and stumbled into the friendly ditch.

Still the planes kept on their course, a little to our left. Would they pass on to the town without seeing the train ? That must be their objective. All would be well yet. No. They were turning, coming round—hell ! Now we were for it.

Silence ! They had shut off their engines. I couldn't see them from my ditch. What was that whistling noise ? Instinctively I put my hands over my head.

A roar and a crash . . . another and another. I crouched lower in the ditch ; crash ! crash ! crash ! . . . closer this time, but still one hundred yards to the right. A roar, and their engines started up again ; they were right over us. My God ! They were bound to hit us. They couldn't miss.

Crash ! crash ! crash ! Too damned close. The smoke and fumes of exploded T.N.T. assailed my nostrils once more. I looked up. Where were they ? They had gone. I breathed a sigh of relief. Where were the others ? Look out ; they were returning right along the train. They would get us this time. Crash ! I was covered with earth and stones, couldn't see for smoke, acrid black smoke. Crash ! Gosh, that was close to the engine ; must have hit it. The drone of their

engines faded, they were going; would they come back?
I lay there shivering. I was in a hell of a funk, and was glad
the others were not near me. I looked up—the noise of their
engines got fainter and fainter—they had gone.

I crawled out of the ditch on to the embankment, where
I found some officers I did not know talking excitedly.
Apparently a bomb had fallen somewhere in front of the
engine, killing the stoker. We were all nervy and strung up.
We had to go back along the train to get the troops aboard.
No one appeared to have been hurt except the wretched
stoker.

After a while the train crawled on again, feeling its way
cautiously towards the town, which turned out to be St. Omer.
We halted once more in the station. I was tired out with the
events of the night, wanted to sleep.

Can we get a drink in this benighted spot? " asked someone.

" What do you think, do you expect the pubs to be open
at this time of night? " laughed Tim.

All this time the men were crowding round the engine with
their mess tins, begging water from the driver to make tea.
We thought we might have some ourselves. It was a bit oily,
but hot.

" Listen ! " said Tim suddenly, spilling his tea.

" Oh, shut up ! " I snapped. " You have got the wind up.
What is it ? "

" Don't you hear them ? "

Someone shouted " lights out." Scurrying feet ran up and
down the platform, and in the distance the " drone, drone "
was coming nearer.

" Blast them ! "

No ditch, no cover. Where could one go? Everyone all
around. I pretended not to mind. Must not panic, had to
stick it in the carriage if the others did. Couldn't very well
get under the seat, although I would have dearly loved to
do so.

" I am not going to sit here," said someone.

" What about under the train ? " said another.

And under the train we went, while the planes roared over
us ; bombs exploded all around us, but not one came within

fifty yards of the train. Buildings crashed, the air was full of smoke ; the stench of burnt explosives filled the air. They dropped six bombs and roared away into the darkness.

Wearily we crept from our place of shelter back to our carriage, too tired to care now if it snowed bombs. I for one was beyond caring. I staggered into the carriage, sat down, and slept.

CHAPTER XII.

ALL QUIET ON THE CAMBRAI FRONT.

SOME hours afterwards I awoke from a troubled sleep to find it was broad daylight, and that the train once more had ceased to function. A wash and a shave were indicated, if water could be obtained. Breakfast was also necessary.

Whittingham arrived with sufficient water from the engine to shave. The others could easily have gone another day without shaving, the advantage of extreme youth.

After this we had breakfast, stale sandwiches and tea. About 10 a.m. we finally stopped at Bapaume, where we detrained.

A dull march over the old Somme battlefields brought us by easy stages to a place called Sorel, on October 10th, where we were once more quartered in a hut encampment.

The days passed uneventfully until October 12th. The Colonel at lunch time told me to come to the orderly room. I went, wondering rather what he wanted to talk about there, as usually we talked things over in the mess.

There was an air of secrecy and of untoward events in the air. My curiosity was aroused and I waited expectantly for the Colonel to notice my presence.

He looked up, so I stood to attention and saluted.

We were alone, Tim had tactfully departed.

He did not speak for a few seconds.

" I leave you to-morrow," he said. " Got a brigade."

" Congratulations, Sir," was all I could say.

It suddenly dawned on me what a wonderful friend he had been, and how I should miss him. I thought of the twelve months I had worked beside him, of his great kindness, of all the small ways in which he had helped me. Everything came back in a rush. He was leaving us. I did not know what to say.

" I am sorry I can't take you with me ; I tried, but it could not be done. However, I have done my best for you," he said. " The General wants you to go to him as Brigade Intelligence Officer. I have given you a good chit."

I was overwhelmed with gratitude.

We talked for a while of old times, but I confess that my feelings were mixed. He had been a wonderful commanding officer and friend at the same time.

We gave him a great farewell dinner that night. The next day he departed in all the glory of red tabs and gold lace. The whole battalion assembled to see him off and gave him a parting cheer.

What a man he was. I did not see him again until after the war, by which time he had collected a C.M.G. and three bars to his D.S.O.

I reported to brigade headquarters the same day.

Brigadier-General Duncan was a regular soldier and a Scotsman. I was a good bit in awe of him for some time, but as I had been at school with Sanderson, the Brigade Major, things were made much easier for me.

Lord Erleigh, the staff-captain, was an ex-civilian like myself, an excellent fellow with a great sense of humour and a very pretty wit. He could make the General laugh at breakfast.

The General's servant was a most excellent cook; his dishes made of tinned salmon were a poem, his repertoire was apparently inexhaustible, as he never seemed to serve it twice alike. The General had a great weakness for tinned salmon. I never touch this fish in tinned form now; my desire for it ended with my departure from France.

Once again I was appointed mess president. It was a job which required a considerable amount of tact.

My quarters now were very much better than they were with the battalion, as I shared a fair-sized room with Sanderson, having a proper iron bedstead with a spring mattress, a washstand, a dressing table, and a table for writing.

My duties, however, were more onerous, as besides having the Intelligence officers under my orders, I had to act as A.D.C. to the General and the Brigade Major, accompanying them on their periodical visits to the line. Of the Staff-Captain I saw very little, except at mess.

The next morning at breakfast I was ordered to accompany

the General up the line at 10 a.m., so having collected
sandwiches and a flask for both of us, I made my way to
his room.

We were then, I suppose, about three miles from the
front line.

We started punctually from our camp. The day was fine
and warm. I noticed that the General took no orderly, but
I said nothing ; also I noticed that he wore no badges on his
tin hat. We both took walking sticks.

We walked for about half a mile down a sunken road before
we arrived in open flat country, rather like Cambridgeshire.
On our left was the village of Trescault, with Havrincourt Wood
beyond it, and the village of Havrincourt itself about two
miles to our left front. This village was just inside our lines.
In front of us stretched uninteresting country, which looked
as if it would yield wonderful wheat crops and partridge
driving.

On the way the General commented on the amount of light-
railway material we saw lying about in dumps. This made
me ask whether we were going to make an attack in these
parts. However, he seemed to know nothing, so I did not
refer to it again. Light railways were a sure sign of offensive
action in the future.

After we had walked about two miles we arrived at the
commencement of the trench system. A wonderful communication trench about seven feet deep and duck-boarded the
whole way led up to the line.

From there we had a good view of the surrounding country,
as we were now on the highest part of a ridge falling away
gradually to Trescault and Havrincourt on the left, and down
to a valley on the right, with the village of Gouzeaucourt
showing plainly on the opposite slope. Beyond this we could
see the village of Gonnelieu and La Vacquerie in the distance.
Immediately in front of us was the village of Villers Plouich,
with a wood on the left of it.

We proceeded along the trench without meeting anyone.
There seemed to be complete quiet, no shells, rifle fire or other
signs of war. After we had walked down what seemed miles
of trench we came upon signs of life and battalion headquarters.

A few men were lounging about when we arrived, but they soon sprang to attention when they caught sight of the General's red tabs.

After walking down about thirty steep steps we came to the main dugout, which the officers used as a mess room and also for work. The Adjutant was busily engaged in writing returns, and the Colonel was reading a book.

Leading off the main dugout was a passage, with bunks arranged in tiers. Here the officers slept in beds with mattresses made of wire netting; the battalion headquarters staff and the signallers had a small room to themselves. Telephone lines ran from here to the companies in the line, and also to brigade in the rear. There was also a quite respectable mess kitchen.

The Colonel rose to greet the General, with whom he shook hands. I talked to the Adjutant, getting as much information from him as I could before we started for the front line. It appeared that they had been there for more than a month, employing most of their time in making the trenches and dugouts as comfortable and safe as possible.

During our tour we were both lost in admiration of their work. The trenches, beautifully planned to give an excellent field of fire, were built up with sandbags, supported with wire netting in the fire bays and round the trenches. The whole of the system was duck-boarded; it was the most perfect system of trenches I saw during the time I was in France.

We inspected the company headquarters and found them in deep dugouts, planned in the same way as battalion headquarters, but of course on a smaller scale.

From the fire step in the front line we had an excellent view of the German lines, which were further off than usual. In fact, in some places No Man's Land was nearly five hundred yards wide.

We were astonished to observe German soldiers walking about within rifle range behind their line. Our men appeared to take no notice. I privately made up my mind to do away with that sort of thing when we took over; such things could not be allowed. These people evidently did not know there was a war on. Both sides apparently believed in the policy " live and let live."

The General and I ignored the communication trench on the return journey. We walked along the top through the rough grass, which grew abundantly, putting up several coveys of partridges *en route*.

On October 14th we relieved the brigade in the line, and for the first time in my experience the relief was carried out in broad daylight, thanks to the wonderful communication trenches.

Orders were sent to battalions that much stricter discipline was to be observed in the line. Men had to shave and keep their kit spotless, etc. This came as a great change to our warlike troops, who were not used to that sort of thing.

The front was so quiet that it was difficult to restrain the men from walking about on the top. Also an order had to be sent to battalions forbidding the men to shoot at game, owing to the likelihood of casualties from spent bullets behind our line.

Our division was holding a very wide front supported by the minimum of artillery, with no heavy guns at all. It stretched from a point north of Beaucamp to the other side of Villers Guislan.

Time passed very peacefully, as the Germans were very quiet. My battalion snipers had the time of their lives ; never before had they been given such targets. We literally kept a game book of hits for the first three days ; after that the Germans did not show themselves so much ; also they started to retaliate.

Wiring was carried out nearly every night, but not in the style we were accustomed to in the days of the Somme. Our men did not creep through the wire carrying coils of wire, stakes, etc. ; instead, a general service wagon was driven into No Man's Land with materials on board, which were dumped out when required. At first we expected bursts of machine gun fire every minute, but nothing happened. It must have become a well-established custom, as the enemy did the same thing themselves ; we did not interfere.

They also had a light railway, which ran from Ribecourt to their front line, as we could frequently hear the train coming up with their rations.

For the moment we were enjoying a quiet and peaceful life. Casualties were rare.

CHAPTER XIII.

PREPARATIONS FOR "THE DAY."

THE first signs of activity started on November 1st with a visit from the corps commander, General Sir W. P. Pulteney and his staff, to our headquarters.

Such important visitors gave me much anxiety about the luncheon menu. However, it passed off to the satisfaction of the General, who was very thoughtful after the subsequent secret meeting. He told us later that he was informed confidentially about the projected attack on the 20th at this meeting.

Soon afterwards materials for light railways made their appearance and preparations began in earnest.

We were not told anything at all about it. Things went on as usual with us until November 6th, when at a meeting after lunch of the officers of the staff we were told, under promise of secrecy, about the forthcoming battle. Various generals and staff officers came to lunch during the next few days, and it was my duty to take them round the line to show them everything they wished to see.

The whole atmosphere of this part of the front now began to change with great rapidity, and scenes of feverish activity prevailed. Ammunition dumps were being formed, artillery officers were reconnoitring new positions for guns ; during each night guns were brought up and covered with camouflage netting.

In Havrincourt Wood the activity was intense. It was simply bristling with guns and troops in bivouac.

It was wonderful luck for everybody concerned that every day from now onwards to the day of the battle it was very misty, so that the German aeroplanes which came over flying very high could see nothing of our preparations ; but I have an idea they knew something was going on, but did not know the real facts.

All these activities, as I said before, had no effect on us, as we were holding the line. We carried on with our daily jobs as if nothing was happening. In fact, up till now the

troops in the line itself (and this included the officers) did not
yet know about the projected attack, or what was going on
in the rear.

On November 8th we received from division the operation
orders and the objective maps for the attack itself, so we
started on the work of preparing orders and objective maps
for the battalions.   This work was done in the greatest secrecy
at night by Sanderson, Erleigh and myself.

All the operation orders were written by Sanderson, and
all the original objective maps for each battalion I did myself.
Erleigh had to work out his orders for rations, ammunition, etc.,
himself, as none of the brigade orderly room staff could be told
at present about the impending battle.

Every day I took officers of divisions who would take part
in the attack up the line to reconnoitre, and by night we
worked in our rooms.

Guns and ammunition were now being moved on to our
front all night, and the noise of traffic and general activity
would have prevented much sleep in any case.   All these
activities died down during the day, so that there should be
no possible chance of any inquisitive German aeroplane
spotting our preparations.

About this time our engineers ran a light railway from
Gouzeaucourt to Villers Plouich, about five hundred men being
employed on this work.   You will hear more about this later,
but I would just at the moment say that this railway was
principally built to feed a battery of 9.2″ howitzers with
ammunition, as this battery was to be placed in the village of
Villers Plouich itself, only two hundred yards behind our front
line.

Our staff ran an enormous risk by doing this, as it was
within easy reach of the German field guns.   If one of their
shells had by any chance fallen in this dump of 9.2″ shells
the result would have been appalling, and the whole show
might have been given away.   However, nothing happened.

On November 15th the colonels and officers of battalions
were called together and given particulars of the attack, and
complicated relief arrangements were made to enable our men
to go to Bray for a day's training with tanks, which very few
of them had seen before.

All the villages and woods now were full of silent guns with their ammunition beside them. Most of them were heavy guns, as the field guns were to come up on the night of the attack itself.

As I told you before, there was a battery of four 9.2" howitzers in Villers Plouich, and also a battery of 4.2" howitzers. These guns, to our great alarm, were fired at by the Germans one night, quite innocently, with trench mortars. I don't suppose that 9.2" howitzers had ever before been near enough to the line to suffer the indignity of being fired at by hostile trench mortars.

On November 16th our operation orders and objective maps were issued to our battalions and our labours for the time being ended. We were able to get a good night's rest for once.

I can remember very well playing bridge one night in mess. Erleigh was making caustic remarks, and the General was not playing too well. I had the nerve to say to him, " Why on earth did you not lead your heart, Sir ? " and then the General started to give us his opinion of civilian officers in the Great War. I can remember him saying, in a joking way, that people like me did not treat him with sufficient respect, and that he could not imagine what would have happened in pre-war days if a mere captain had criticised his general's play at bridge. Also he gave us all a certain amount of praise, because he said he considered it wonderful that out of all his officers in the brigade he and Sanderson were the only two regulars.

The precautions for preventing movement of our troops and transport by day were now redoubled, as all the area up to the front line was now stiff with dumps, railways, guns, etc., all carefully camouflaged so that there should be no risk of the Germans seeing them.

The plan of attack was as follows.

The 12th division was to attack from a line east of Gonnelieu to the centre of the village of La Vacquerie ; the 20th division was to attack from that point to the railway line, and the 6th division from the railway line to the road by Boar Copse. Therefore our present divisional front on the day of the attack was to be reinforced by two divisions, and our division would be squashed in between the other two.

The 20th division received orders to attack the first three objectives with two brigades, and the right brigade and reserve brigade were ordered to form a defensive flank in conjunction with the 12th division facing east. The famous 29th division, commanded by General de Lisle, was in reserve ; they were ordered to be ready at a moment's notice to advance through the lines of the 20th and 6th divisions, and to press forward the attack. More later on about the doings of the 29th division.

A complete corps was placed at the disposal of the army commander as a reserve. Part of this was used afterwards at Bourlon Wood, and had a very bad time there.

The cavalry received orders to be in readiness to act at any time. On the night before the attack they were brought up to a point near Fins and moved up to the line on the day of of the battle, at about 11 a.m.

This was another quiet day with a thick mist.

On November 17th the preparations for the battle seemed to be almost complete, and there was little movement by day.

That night the Germans began to get nervous. Presumably they must have heard the noise we made, which made them think we were making preparations for something opposite their front.

At about 11 p.m. they opened a heavy trench mortar and field gun barrage on our positions opposite Havrincourt Wood, at the same time sending over a company to raid our lines. The noise of this bombardment caused great alarm everywhere behind our lines. We thought that the Bosche was going to make an attack on us, which would have been fatal ; they would have certainly found out about the projected attack on the 20th.

However, in three-quarters of an hour the gun fire ceased and we breathed freely again ; but reports soon came through with the worst possible news, that the Germans had succeeded in the raid and had taken six of our men prisoners. We were filled with anxiety as to what the German Intelligence officers would be able to extract from our men in the way of information about our forthcoming attack. As a matter of fact we heard afterwards that these men of ours only told the Germans that we were going to make a small raid with tanks, so no harm was done.

The higher command was faced with considerable difficulty in massing troops for this attack, owing to the openness of the country, so they adopted a most ingenious device. They covered the hollows in the large fields with the same camouflage I have mentioned before, only on a vast scale. In one instance they levelled the hollow between two quite substantial hillocks with this netting, and underneath it a complete brigade was in camp. All the while the weather still remained foggy, which was tremendous luck.

I was given a responsible post for the duration of the attack.

The brigade intelligence officers of the 6th division were unfamiliar with this part of the front, and therefore they would be very much handicapped during the attack. A meeting was therefore called at our brigade headquarters at which the general officer commanding the 6th division was present, and they decided that the intelligence reports during the battle and the observation posts should be placed under my supervision. I was to be in charge of the Intelligence Department of the entire 6th division as well as of the 60th brigade, a post of very great responsibility. As this was sprung on me three days before the battle itself I had very little time to prepare my plans.

I called a meeting of the brigade intelligence officers of the 6th division and arranged for a central observation post to be built on the higher ground opposite Villers Plouich. This I should occupy myself during the battle. Also it was arranged that I should have a system of telephonic communication with the other posts which were already in existence, and which would be occupied during the battle by officers from the 6th division.

In case the telephone wires were broken by shell fire each observation post would be supplied with runners to take messages.

It was arranged for all messages to be sent in the first place to me, and that I should have the responsibility of sorting them out and reporting the progress of the battle to 6th divisional headquarters, and also to General Duncan commanding the 60th brigade.

Needless to say I was very pleased to be given such responsibility.

On November 18th an order was issued that officers and men of the 6th division should be made familiar with the ground that they were about to attack, and therefore two brigades took over our front from Boar Copse to the railway, leaving the troops of the 60th brigade to hold the outpost or front line only.

Our men had been in the line through all the hectic preparations in the rear, and although they may have suspected a lot their actual knowledge was very small. Therefore the powers that be considered that they should still remain in the outpost or front line until the night of the attack, in case the Germans made another raid. These men were ordered to rejoin their units on the night before the attack, and the 60th brigade then took over six hundred yards front on the right of the railway.

This day again was very misty, but a really exciting incident took place. A German aeroplane flying very low came over our back areas two miles behind the line in the fog, and was shot down by one of our Lewis guns. Once again we breathed a sigh of relief. The flying officer was captured intact, and the Intelligence Department discovered that he had lost his way and had no idea of the part of the front he was flying over. He was carefully looked after.

On this day we had our first view of the tanks in any quantities, and astonishing sights they were. We had all seen tanks before at Ypres, but I am afraid our opinion of them was not very high, as they invariably got stuck in the mud. But as the weather was very fine they seemed to get along quite easily, although they made a dreadful noise.

As we looked on at the crews moving them about, and listened to the shouting that took place, the clankings and roar of the engines, etc., we could quite imagine what would happen when about four hundred of them approached the front line.

More of this later.

On the tops of them they carried objects which looked like bundles of faggots tied together with wire. We could not make out what on earth these things were for. We were told, however, that they were called 'facines,' which could be automatically pulled forward over the nose of the tank and dropped into a trench which was too deep to negotiate without the use of them.

Meanwhile, in the trenches, the traverses were flattened out where the tanks were to pass over, and arrangements were made for guiding the tanks up to the point from which they were going to make the attack.

That night the enemy made another raid on our right battalion after a violent trench mortar barrage. They managed to take one prisoner, and we heard from German officers afterwards that this man disclosed nothing about the forth-coming attack.

November 19th, known to us all as ' Y ' day, was still misty. It was a day of feverish activity. Last instructions were being carried out.

The General and I proceeded to visit the line by ourselves, without orderlies, and during this walk quite an amusing incident took place. The General was the sort of man who liked to go up to various men to ask them what they were doing. On this occasion he saw some men putting up telephone posts and laying lines. These men were at least a mile behind our front line. The General asked them what they were doing, whereupon they informed him that they were signallers and that they were laying telephone lines up to headquarters. He asked one fellow if he had ever been in the front line, and he replied that " he hoped his duty would never take him that far." The General was speechless, even his power of repartee failed him. All that he could say was, "And to think that that man was a Scotsman." The General was a Scotsman himself.

Each battalion was to attack with eighteen tanks, and the tanks were to advance in groups of three in the form of a triangle. There were six groups of tanks attacking in a line with each battalion.

There were supply tanks, tanks especially equipped with wire-cutting apparatus, and several which had a roving commission, *i.e.*, the commander had orders to keep his eyes open, and to chip in if he saw any of our troops in difficulties.

There were four hundred and seven tanks employed in this battle.

This was the first time in the war that we had ever attempted a large surprise attack against a very powerful line of trenches such as the Hindenburg Line. In front of us there were no less than three rows of intact wire. None of our artillery had been registered before the battle, and the gunners could therefore only fire by the map.

It was arranged that all the wire cutting and flattening should be done by the tanks, and that the infantry should follow behind them through the wire. At 8 p.m. we finished our last meal, so I proceeded up the line with the faithful Whittingham. At 9 p.m. word was sent back to brigade headquarters that all the troops were in their positions, and I went across to our battle headquarters in Villers Plouich. About this time there was a little hostile shelling, but very little more than usual. The night was quiet.

At midnight a continuous roar in the distance informed us that the tanks were moving up to their positions. Everybody was in a dither of excitement. The noise of their approach got louder and louder ; minute by minute our anxiety increased, as we could not think it possible that the enemy could help hearing the outrageous noise they were making.

As they approached their positions in the dark the guides in front were shouting directions at the top of their voices. We were expecting every minute the German batteries to open up along the whole front line with all the guns they could bring to bear.

The tank close to me made the most shattering noise. It seemed to have an open exhaust and the captain, or whoever he was in charge, seemed to have no realisation of his close proximity to the enemy. However, he got the great hulk into its allotted position, and at last stopped his engine, and still nothing happened. This time I suppose it was about 3 a.m. in the morning. Desultory firing was still going on from both sides, but from now onwards the night was calm. All activity seemed to have ceased. I tried to snatch an hour or two's sleep before ' Zero ' started at 6-30 a.m.

The observation post was placed behind the front line on

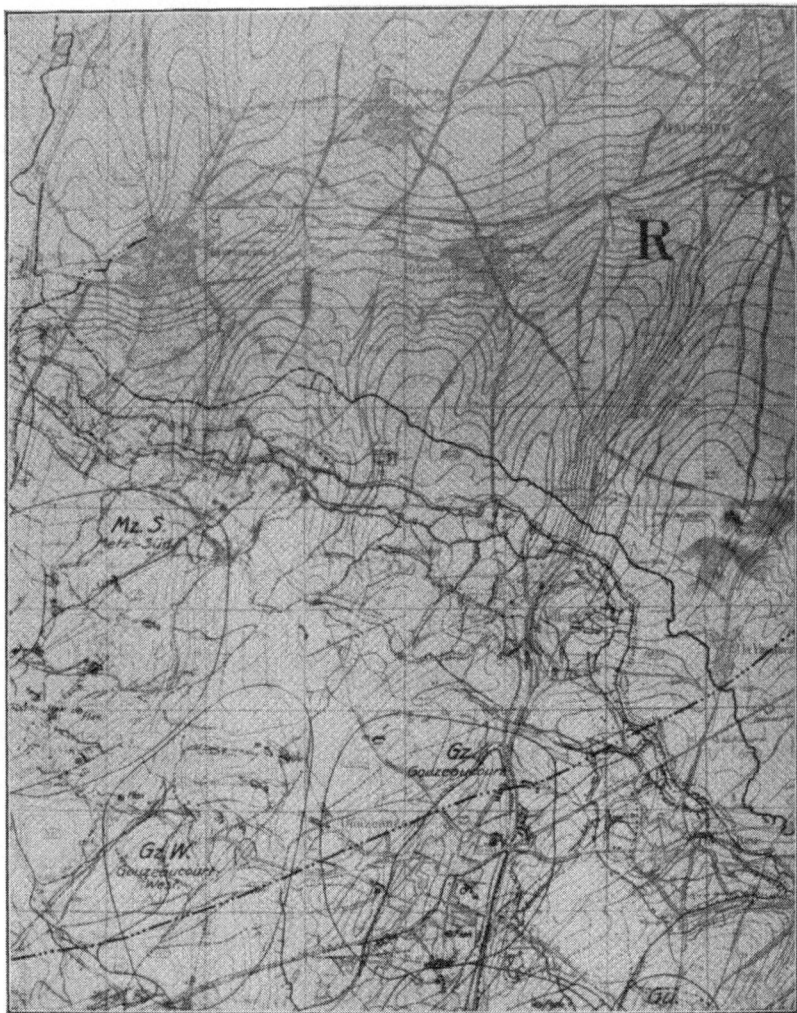

German Artillery Map of our organisations before the
Battle of Cambrai.

the highest spot that we could find, and in a position which would give us a very fine view of the country behind the enemy lines. It was very carefully constructed and covered over with sandbags and corrugated iron. The top was carefully camouflaged so that the German aeroplanes could not see it.

To our left front we had a good view of No Man's Land, with Boar Copse in the middle. In the distance we could see a long way over the German lines where the country was flat.

Immediately in front of us, and at about a distance of five hundred yards was the German wire and the first Hindenburg line trench system.

The ground behind this sloped down to the village of Ribecourt. Of this we could only see the tops of the roofs. This village lay in a valley, and behind it the ground sloped up gradually to the Flesquieres Ridge, which extended along the whole of our immediate front, and behind which the Germans' heavy batteries were placed. They were, of course, out of sight.

Behind this, in the distance, a few miles away, the ground sloped up, culminating on the horizon with Bourlon Village and Bourlon Wood. On our half-right front the ground sloped downwards to a valley in which lay the village of Villers Plouich, inside our lines. This valley extended through the German Hindenburg Line till it reached the valley extending from left to right. At the far end of this valley lay the canal Du Nord, and the villages of Masnieries and Marcoing. We could see Marcoing, and beyond it up a slope which continued for miles towards Cambrai. In the distance was the village of Romilly, but we could only see a small portion of the village of Masnieries, which lay on the far bank of the canal.

Towards our right, and over the valley, there was a ridge which extended as far back as the village of La Vacquerie. This ridge, which extended right across the German lines, limited our view to the right. The ridge was about one and a half miles away from our observation post.

CHAPTER XIV.

The Battle of Cambrai.

At 6 a.m. it was beginning to grow light, sounds of great activity could be heard on all sides. Tank engines were being started up, the noise alarming us very much. We expected that before they were ready to start the German barrage would open up and upset things.

As the time grew nearer our anxiety increased, but nothing happened.

At 6-30 a.m. all the guns behind us opened at once with a deafening crash.

The tanks started to move forward to the attack, followed by our troops.

I had not seen any plans for the artillery barrage, but arrangements must have been made for a large quantity of smoke shells to be fired, so that our tanks could not be seen by the Germans until they were actually upon them.

For quite an appreciable time, therefore, we could see very little of what was going on, owing to the smoke screen ; but we could hear the machine guns and small artillery which the tanks carried firing from our front.

The troops following the tanks disappeared into the smoke, so for the moment we had little or nothing to do. For five minutes or so the German artillery did not reply ; they then opened on our front line a very heavy shell fire, which compelled us to seek the shelter of our deep dugouts for a few minutes.

At 6-50 we came up to our post again. We could see that our tanks and troops had reached the first Hindenburg Line, and were pressing through it. This was duly reported to headquarters.

For some time after this there was nothing much to report owing to smoke, but it cleared about 7-30 a.m., and from what we could see the troops on our right were held up near a place called Goodman's Farm.

About this time the first German prisoners arrived. We questioned them, and some of them who could speak a little

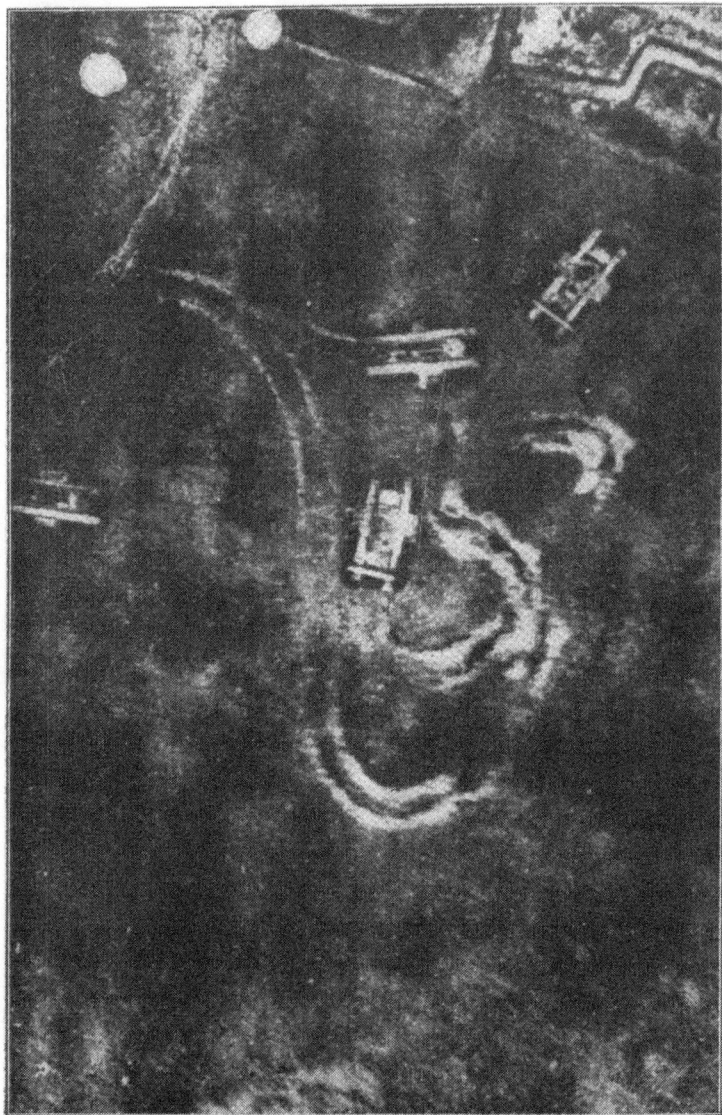

Photograph of our Tanks in action at the Battle of Cambrai, taken by a German airman on November 20th, 1917.

(*By courtesy of the Imperial War Museum. Copyright Reserved.*)

English told us that our surprise was absolutely complete, and that they had had no idea there was going to be an attack on such a scale.

The German officers whom we interviewed were not a pleasant lot ; they were rather like the typical German officers one reads about in books and sees on the pictures.

One rather terrible thing happened at this time. One of our fellows came back behaving as if he was completely mad. He was gibbering and foaming at the mouth. I am afraid that he was a very bad case of shell shock.

At 8 a.m. we sent down a report to brigade and to divisional headquarters that we could see that the first Hindenburg system was completely captured all along our front, that the tanks and troops were advancing towards their second line of trenches, and that everything appeared to be going well.

About this time the enemy appeared to be completely demoralised ; prisoners were pouring in.

An officer prisoner stated that they had expected an attack near Havrincourt. They had learned about this from the statements of our prisoners taken in a raid. He also told me that the Germans were preparing to make an attack on this sector themselves, and that the billets in the local villages had all been allotted to their storm troops.

About 9-40 a.m. all the German shelling appeared to have ceased. We viewed the battle from the top of our observation post ; behind us great activity prevailed ; for the first time we saw the magnificent spectacle of our field artillery limbering up and going forward, first at the trot, then at the gallop, battery after battery, to take up new positions on the captured German front line.

This was the first time that we had ever seen the artillery moving forward. It gave us all a great thrill ; this attack of ours seemed to be developing into a great victory.

At the same time the 29th division behind us received orders to go through to attack our last objectives. As far as we could see on the right they marched, three brigades in line, each battalion in fours. I cannot describe in words what a wonderful sight it was. The only thing missing was a band in front of each battalion. We cheered.

Battery after battery of artillery moved off at a gallop to take up new positions. The special tanks for clearing the wire trundled up and down the Hindenburg Line catching up the wire with hooks and rolling it into huge balls, so that it should not get in the way of our cavalry, who were to come up shortly.

At 10-40 a.m. we could see our tanks and troops entering the village of Marcoing ; also we could see in front of us the tanks advancing towards the top of the Flesquieres Ridge ; we could see that the village of Flesquieres had not yet fallen. This was most important news, so a message was sent to division and headquarters to acquaint the Generals of this fact. It meant that we were right through the Hindenburg Line, and advancing into the open country beyond.

General Duncan told me afterwards that this message was so incredible, that so far as he was concerned he sent it forward adding a note to say he could hardly believe it. I think the powers that be waited for this information to be confirmed before they ordered the cavalry forward. In fact, it was not until 12-30 p.m. that the cavalry received orders to advance.

All this time we could see our troops digging in to make their positions secure. The Flesquieres Ridge in front of us was a wonderful sight, shells bursting in all directions. Many tanks at this time were on fire on the ridge, the German batteries firing at them almost at point blank range.

Near the village of Villers Plouich we could see masses of men working hard constructing a light railway and repairing the roads for our transport and heavy guns to come up.

About this time the first of the cavalry started to arrive, and a wonderful sight they were. Regiment after regiment passed us going down the valley on our right. When they got behind the lines occupied by our troops they dismounted, waiting for orders under cover. By their arrival it looked as if we were going to make a push right through to the rear of the German lines ; but more of this later.

Motor machine gun corps and cyclists were also pushing forward, and at about 1 o'clock squadrons of the cavalry passed through the front of the 29th division to capture the two villages of Cantaing and Noyelles, which lay more than four miles behind the original German line.

By this time civilians from the villages of Marcoing and Masnieries were coming back through our lines, carrying what possessions they could save on their backs, driving cows and pigs in front of them.

This was the first time that any of us had taken part in such a victory. We felt exalted.

At 2 p.m., having given orders that all our observation posts should be evacuated, I went forward to see the General. We took a walk round the line, visiting our future brigade headquarters, which was a fine dugout in the second system of the Hindenburg Line. This dugout was marvellous. Very deep and furnished with feather beds, chairs, tables, etc., which the Germans had evidently looted from neighbouring villages.

We had some food and drank some excellent lager beer.

After lunch I went on a tour of inspection with Whittingham.

The first thing we came to was a German field battery, every gun out of action with the exception of one. By this was lying a single German officer, quite dead. In front of him were five tanks, which he had evidently succeeded in knocking out himself, single-handed, with his gun. A brave man. I believe this officer was mentioned for his bravery in our Army Orders that night, which was almost unprecedented.

Lost in admiration of the wonderful Hindenburg system of trenches, we came to a complete anti-aircraft battery, which appeared to be quite intact. We found some of our gunners trying to turn round a battery of German guns so that they could fire them at the Germans themselves. A party of our men were watching the proceedings in silence.

Looking down the barrel of one I found that I could not see through it, so I asked the man who was going to load it what was in the barrel. He said, " There is a shell stuck in it. We will soon get it out."

I mentioned that the gun was pointing to the rear towards Villers Plouich, but he seemed to think it was pointing in the right direction ; also he said he was going to fire it.

Quickly and speedily all the spectators drifted away to places of safety to await results. The man fired the gun, and much to our astonishment the gun did not burst.

We then continued our walk down the Hindenburg Line; here we found one of the German artillery observation posts wonderfully fitted up with an elaborate range-finding apparatus. We seized all the maps we could find in this dugout.

There appeared to be no Germans left at all. Everybody was walking about on the top and in front of our front line doing just as they liked.

Down one dugout we found a German battalion canteen, but a lot of our troops had got there first. It was obvious that our presence was very badly needed. The canteen was full of every kind of drink, from beer to brandy. Luckily the men who had discovered this canteen were men of my old battalion, so I asked two of them to collect all the brandy in sandbags, which we took to headquarters. We also took with us a large quantity of butter and cheese. We left the beer for the men to drink. They had earned it.

At 2-30 p.m. a report came from the 29th division that a small party of the enemy were holding the village of Romilly. The cavalry were ordered up to take it amidst terrific excitement.

We could see them going through the outskirts of Masnieres, but apparently they were held up because a tank had tried to cross the bridge, crashing into the canal. However, numbers of the cavalry managed to get round this obstacle, and making an attack on foot captured the village.

A squadron which we did not see went right out into the country, actually entering Cambrai itself.

At 4-30 p.m. that afternoon most of the cavalry returned.

I was told afterwards that a meeting of the cavalry commanders was held at our brigade headquarters, when they decided " that the time for cavalry had not yet arrived."

We could not understand this as we had penetrated the enemy positions to a depth of four miles. We could only think that the general officer commanding the cavalry was still in his headquarters, thirty-six miles away.

Captain Cox, Brigade Major of the 3rd Tank brigade, rode into Marcoing in the afternoon to see how things were going. He was received unofficially in the village by a fair lady of uncertain age and large proportions, who threw her arms round his neck and kissed him, much to his embarrassment. She evidently regarded him as the first of the victorious British.

Outside her house, which stood on a four-cross road, was a tank, the commander of which was enquiring the way from the inhabitants.

Captain Cox ordered it to turn round, as it was going in the wrong direction.

There was little room for the unwieldly creature to manœuvre, but by dint of revolving on its own axis it managed to get round, but in doing so the rear part of it hit the corner of the house in which Captain Cox's lady friend lived. Only about two feet of brickwork was removed and all seemed well.

Cox was busy directing the tank. He did not see that the brickwork was crumbling. Bricks and rubble were falling fast ; then, with a roar like an avalanche, the whole corner of the house fell into the street.

Yelling imprecations in French the lady rushed at Captain Cox and boxed his ears with both hands. He retreated with as much dignity as the circumstances would allow. He was deaf for days.

After tea at 5 p.m. I went out by myself from brigade headquarters along the Hindenburg Line, as my orders were to report our position to the brigade on our right.

By this time it was getting dark. It was a pretty grim job struggling down the trenches, tumbling over dead Germans, especially as I had no notion where the headquarters were. However I managed to find them, and at about 9-30 p.m. I got back very tired.

The General told me the result of our magnificent victory.

We had captured 9,774 prisoners, 123 guns, 79 trench mortars and 281 machine guns.

CHAPTER XV.

NERVES.

WE were absolutely exhausted. I wanted to go to bed, but before I could get there I was sent for by the General, who told me I should have to go round the line with him at 6 a.m. the following morning.

I told his orderly to call us at 5-30 a.m., also that the General and I would require food and tea. . . . I suppose I did not get to my bed, which was very comfortable, until about 2 a.m.

I woke up again to find that it was five minutes to six. No one had called me. I was extremely angry.

I shouted for Whittingham and asked him why he had not done so. He told me that he had received no orders. I sent for the General's orderly. He also told me that he had received no orders to call me. I told him he was a —— liar, and that I had given him instructions to call me and the General before I had gone to bed. This he denied, and told me that he would report what I had said to the General.

When I had dressed I went into the mess for breakfast to find a stony silence. The General at once asked me if it was true that I had called his man a —— liar. He repeated the words I was supposed to have said.

I replied that the man was a liar, and that I had told him so.

The General then told me that as I had said this he would have to interview me in the presence of his orderly, which he proceeded to do.

I could see that the General was very upset.

The man repeated the words I had said to him, which I could not deny. When the man had said what he had got to say the General sent him out of the mess, and proceeded to very nicely tell me off. I was of course standing to attention all this time. I don't know whether it was the strain of the past few days that caused my nerves to give way suddenly, but to the horror of the General I burst into tears and wept for half an hour without stopping. This alarmed the General to such an extent that he did not know what to do with me. He was fearfully upset, and for the time being the incident blew over.

When we got out of the line he was very kind about it, and nothing unpleasant happened. In fact, he was good enough to put forward my name to go for a rest to the south of France.

On the next day, the 21st of November, the troops on our left made an attack on Bourlon Wood, capturing it, but the attack on Crevoecour, on our right, was not successful, and the Germans still continued to hold the bridge over the canal.

Cavalry went off at dawn on this day, but were held up by scattered machine gun posts, which evidently had been brought up in the night.

Our line was now in the form of a very acute salient, as our attack had only been on a front of about seven miles. We had penetrated about four miles deep into the German lines. Therefore we had two flanks to defend, which were very much open to German counter-attack.

The 12th division on our right were facing one of these flanks ; our front extended from Crevoecour along the canal bank to within a quarter of a mile of Masnieries ; from there the 29th division held the line.

Our left flank ended by a bridge over the canal on our side ; on the other side of this bridge the 29th division held the front.

Our brigade headquarters by this time had been moved over the ridge into a sunken road north of La Vacquerie, and a very comfortable dugout it was.

We were not relieved after the attack as we expected to be ; the men had no overcoats and the weather was very cold. It was also very difficult to provide the troops with hot food, therefore their spirits became rather low as time went on, especially as prospects of relief were dim. We could see in front of us our divisional artillery formed up in a huge horse shoe, facing our front, which was very much to a flank.

An incident happened one windy night which was very unfortunate. The point where our brigade joined up with the 29th division, as I have said before, was situated at the canal bank, and at this our extreme left flank we had a Lewis gun post. One windy night the men in charge of this post heard people coming towards them from the other bank of the canal. They challenged them and received no reply, so they opened fire with the Lewis guns, with disastrous results. It turned out that they had fired at officers of the 29th division. Some of them were wounded ; I believe one was killed.

It was my unfortunate duty to go to their headquarters in Marcoing the next day to explain what had happened, and to express the regrets of my General. I was received in utter silence, and it was a most distressing episode altogether.

There is very little to relate about the next few days. We spent the time in consolidating our line as best we could. The General and staff made many visits to our front, and under the unpleasant circumstances we did our best to make the men comfortable. It was the end of November and the weather was wet and cold ; the trenches were newly dug and the men had no dugouts to sleep in. The difficulty of supplying them with hot food became a serious matter, and I am afraid in consequence the morale of the troops was badly shaken.

My particular duty during these days was to get my brigade observers into positions from which they could see behind the German lines. I therefore constructed one observation post on the top of the ridge overlooking Crevoecour and another on the ridge behind us. Both were in communication with our brigade headquarters in the sunken road by telephone.

During these days, up to the 29th of November, there were many signs of German activity behind their lines. The observers sent messages to inform us that they had seen troops being brought up by motor buses ; also one afternoon the Germans opened up a barrage on our right near Lateau Wood. This looked very like a practice barrage for an attack.

Meanwhile the powers that be apparently ignored these portents of the events which followed.

Our Tanks passing captured guns at Graincourt on their way to attack Bourlon Wood on November 23rd, 1917. G Battalion, 40th Division.

CHAPTER XVI.

THE DEBACLE.

WE had received orders from division that our brigade would be relieved on the night of the 29th–30th November by the 61st brigade. Orders were therefore sent out to battalions that this relief would take place, as far as our battalions were concerned, in the evening, and that it was to be completed by 11 p.m. on the night of the 29th. The 61st brigade staff were to relieve us at 8 a.m. on the morning of the 30th, so that from 11 p.m. on the night of the 29th we were nominally in command of the 61st brigade, who were holding the line.

" Relief complete " was reported at 11-30 p.m., and we did not know for certain the names of the battalion commanders of the 61st brigade who were now holding the line.

The night was very quiet and dawn broke misty. At 6-45 a.m. we were aroused by a very heavy bombardment, which we could see was taking place north of us in the direction of Bourlon Wood ; an attack was developing there. As this was not on our front we took no notice and went down to complete our breakfast, which luckily was finished just before 7 a.m. At 7 a.m. to the minute a very intense barrage from the German artillery started on our front line, and although we were quite a mile and a half away from it the noise of the exploding shells was deafening.

I was at once ordered by the General to go up to the top of the dugout to investigate what was happening. Erleigh came with me.

A tear gas shell dropped very close to us immediately we had arrived at the top of the stairs. We wept. Owing to the smoke and shells which were now falling around us we could not see the front, but we could hear our artillery firing as quickly as they could load the guns.

We reported this to the General, who, while we had been away, had been trying to get into telephonic communication with our forward positions and with the battalions. There was no reply. No message came from my forward observation post. The line was dead.

Very soon after this the Germans lengthened their range ; their barrage was now concentrated just in front of the sunken road where we were. I was ordered by the General to proceed at once to my observation post in the rear as best I could. When I got there an astonishing sight met my eyes. On our brigade front I could see our troops retreating with the Germans following them. The enemy were then amongst our batteries, which were arranged, as I said before, in a large half-circle facing east.

I immediately telephoned to brigade headquarters giving a report of what I had seen. I also informed the General that he must evacuate brigade headquarters with the utmost speed, as the Germans were not more than three hundred yards away.

I then proceeded with one man to try to collect some of the stragglers who were by this time pouring back, to form some sort of a line to hold up the German attack. I went up to one party of about twenty in charge of a sergeant, and to my amazement I found that they had no rifles. They had dropped them.

The reserve battalion was holding a line on the ridge behind us, and from what I could see the rest of the brigade and all our artillery had been captured already. I therefore went further back over the top of the ridge, where I found in a dugout the headquarters of a labour company of the Durham Light Infantry. The officer in charge was an excellent fellow. He said he would collect his company at once, so I told him to place himself and his men under the command of the reserve battalion, which was still on the ridge, and that if he did not find them to hold the line on the left.

All this time the German shell fire was very intense. Their aeroplanes were very active indeed, flying over our lines in large numbers very low. They were shooting with machine guns at the troops on the ground, and I am quite sure that this did more to demoralise our men than anything else. Several times we had to lie down in a convenient shell hole and shiver while the observer in the aeroplane over us plastered the ground around us with machine gun bullets.

In my search for reinforcements I went further down the valley north of Villers Plouich, and there I found a large party of men under an officer, who were busy building a railway line in the direction of Marcoing. They had with them a complete train of open trucks and the engine had steam up. I approached the officer in charge, asking him to immediately fall in his men so that I could guide them up the line to reinforce our front. Also I told him that this was urgent as our line had been broken through. As soon as I had said this the whole crowd bolted for the train, without any delay jumped into the trucks, and the train started off in the direction of Gouzeau-court ; they had no rifles.

I was told afterwards that this train went straight into the middle of Gouzeaucourt, which was at that time held by the Germans. They left the train hurriedly and I expect they had a pretty thin time.

I then went back to the line to find that the General and his staff were in the front line with the reserve battalion, and that the advance for the time being was held up.

I then received orders from the General to proceed to divisional headquarters at once and inform General Douglas Smith as to what had happened and to ask for his instructions.

The scene at divisional headquarters at Villers Plouich was sensational. There were crowds of officers from the division on our right, many of them in a state of undress, but although it was reported at the time that these officers were caught in their pyjamas I did not see any myself ; the General received me in his dugout perfectly calmly. He said he was very pleased to see me ; would I have a cup of tea ? He also said that as far as the 61st brigade was concerned he had no idea where they were, and he would be very glad if I would tell him something about them. I did my best to explain what had happened, and showed him our position on the map.

He gave me instructions to tell General Duncan to hang on to the positions we were now holding, and that he would do his best to send us reinforcements. He also suggested that General Duncan should send a messenger to the 29th division, who were not being attacked, to see if he could borrow a battalion to come to our support.

At 9 a.m. I returned to the top of the ridge, and from there I had a wonderful view of the counter-attack made by the 60th brigade and the Guards. They put up a wonderful show, driving the Germans out of Gouzeaucourt and part of Gonnelieu. We were told afterwards that if the Germans had persevered with the attack in this direction they would have been able to cut off all our troops who were holding the Bourlon and Marcoing region. An S.O.S. at this time was sent for the the cavalry to come to the rescue. Their arrival gave us great encouragement and was a magnificent sight. They dismounted and came into the battle as infantry.

The scene behind our line at this time almost beggars description. As far as we could see transport of every kind was making off across country as hard as it could go. Engineers were blowing up dumps all over the place, and heavy guns which were now quite close to the front line were being dismantled or being got ready to be blown up.

Our machine gun officer told me afterwards about their part in the affair. The Machine Gun Corps left their ammunition in the line for the relieving company to take over. This, of course, was to save the heavy labour of carting the boxes of ammunition backwards and forwards up the line. Our machine gun company got to their quarters after their relief, but were unable to find the ammunition depot, therefore they had ten perfectly good machine guns without any ammunition. When the Germans attacked in the early hours of the morning these machine guns were therefore more or less useless. But the officer commanding the company was not to be beaten. Deciding that the very look of them might upset the Germans, he placed all his guns in a row in a prominent position and ordered his men to fire ' rapid ' with their rifles. This bluff effectively stopped the German advance in this vicinity.

The attack seemed to be fading away owing to the lack of cohesion amongst the Germans. The officers did not appear to know what to do when they had got out of touch with their seniors, and it looked as if the entire attack had been held up. However, we were holding on with literally our last reserves, and at 3 p.m. I was sent by the General to look for supports, as he told me at this time that there were only five hundred of the brigade left.

Very foolishly I went towards the back areas without an

orderly with me, as I had no idea at that time where the battalions of the 29th division were situated. However, I eventually found a battalion of the Sherwoods near our old front line ; they were very good and gave me something to eat. Their Colonel told me that he could not do anything without orders from his senior officer, and that I should have to go to Ribecourt to see the General. He gave me a guide to show me the way, so I finally found them in the cellars of one of the houses there. The General gave me a note to the Colonel of the Sherwoods, telling me to go back and inform him that he should place himself under my General's command. As soon as I came out of the cellar the Germans started to shell the village with very heavy guns, which I think were 8". They were dropping all around in the direction I had to go, so I simply took to my heels and ran back as hard as ever I could. The effect of shell fire was far more alarming amongst buildings than out in the open.

The Colonel at once gave orders to his battalion to get ready, and very soon we marched off to report to our General, who was greatly relieved to be able to evacuate the front line. He therefore took up his headquarters in a dugout a short way behind, and for quite a long time things were quiet.

About 6-30 p.m. we were having a scratch sort of meal, consisting of bully beef, bread and butter and tea, when an orderly came in to say that a German soldier had been found wandering about. The General ordered him to be brought in, as he could speak German.

The poor old German was brought in literally shivering with fear, and from what the General told us he seemed to imagine that he was going to be shot immediately. However, the General calmed down his fears, telling the mess orderly to bring him a cup of tea and something to eat. The German soldier was quite disarmed by this (to him) amazing treatment. He thanked the General most profusely, told him he was a Bavarian, and that he had lost his way. He informed the General that the German attack had appeared to be a complete surprise to our troops, that they had surrendered almost at once, and had suffered very few casualties. He said he had seen many of our prisoners, who were being well treated by the Bavarians.

There were many stories going about with regard to the division that had their headquarters in Gouzeaucourt. We were told that the General only just escaped, and that one of the staff who was wounded actually remained in his dugout the whole time the Germans were in occupation of the village.

The Germans lost the opportunity of a very great victory because their junior officers were inexperienced, and also because their men, instead of keeping together, spent a lot of their time looting.

The deeds of valour during the great German counter-attack on the 30th were many, and one of the officers in our division got the V.C. for fighting his gun when all the rest of his men had been killed.

Whittingham did a very great deed on the night of the 30th. It was suddenly discovered that I had left my attache case with all the money belonging to the mess in our old dugout. He had the nerve to go back there that night and retrieve it, although it was quite a long way in front of our front line.

We played bridge in the dugout that night. The General thought that it would be good for us to relax after the events of the day.

During this trying day the General had shown us an example of coolness and cheerfulness hard to beat. Usually he was inclined to be dour; people were rather frightened of him.

All that day he had moved amongst the officers and men in the front line with his staff, joking and laughing with everyone. The hidden character of the man came out when things were at their worst; he set a magnificent example to all of us.

The remains of the division were relieved on December 3rd, embussing near Sorel for a destination further north. We suspected that we were destined for the salient again, as we eventually arrived at Lynde after a tiring railway journey.

Here we spent some weeks before we were fit for use in the line again.

CHAPTER XVII.

THE SALIENT.

MY short experience of the Ypres front had been confined to a period in August and September, 1917. Therefore I was not enthusiastic when I was told we were to go to Dickebusch.

Many were the tales I had been told of the horrors of the salient by those who had been there in 1915.

By this time my nerves were in a state of exhaustion, although my general health was excellent.

On December 16th we went into billets at Dickebusch. Soon afterwards we moved into the line opposite Gheluvelt, astride the Menin Road.

Brigade headquarters stayed for a night or two in the ramparts at Ypres on the way to our final headquarters at Jackdaw tunnels.

Exploring the ruins of the town our thoughts were taken back to the days of 1914 and 1915, when life was dangerous here. Now it was comparatively safe. Ypres was a ruin, and the gaunt remains of the Cloth Hall would be a monument for all time. The ramparts were a warren of dugouts, lived in by a succession of soldiers since 1914.

" Hell Fire Corner " and " The Menin Gate " were on the direct route to our headquarters. Names that will go down to history.

Leaving the Menin Gate we walked as far as Hell Fire Corner, where shells no longer crashed on transport furiously driven past this death trap, and so on to Sanctuary Wood of immortal memory, now deserted, once the scene of bloody fighting. Through this wood our old front line stretched, overlooked by Clapham Junction, a hill not half a mile beyond. We wondered how our men lived in such an overlooked position. We reached our headquarters, an old dugout constructed by the enemy, big enough to hold our brigade headquarters and a complete battalion besides, full of water and smells—airless damp smells.

The relief was completed and the General ordered me to accompany him up the line the next day.

" Shall we take orderlies, Sir ? " I asked.

" No ! " he replied.   You and I will go alone at 7 a.m."

Up the duckboards called ' E ' track, pausing on Clapham Junction, we looked over the whole of the salient.   In the distance now a circle of star shells rose and fell.   They were once miles closer to Ypres—we had done a little ourselves to push them further back—on to the Menin Road, straight as a die for miles.   We did not hang about here.   A machine gun was trained down it, liable to open fire any minute.   On along the duckboards, rather broken here by fresh shells ;   we increased our pace to pass this spot quickly.   The smell of burnt T.N.T. was still fresh.

Past the big trench mortar emplacement, and out into the open ;   only half a mile from the line now.

It was growing light, the duckboard track could be seen by the enemy, but we both decided they would not shell two people.   We made a mistake, because they started at once to shell the duckboards with whizz bangs.

We separated on each side of the duckboards, walking two hundred yards apart on each side.   Unpleasant going, but we preferred the bad walking to the danger of the falling shells.

Reaching battalion headquarters we had breakfast with Colonel Welsh, of the Shropshires ; afterwards the others were visited.

We returned in time for lunch.

This was routine work, which went on for weeks.

American officers came to us for instruction ;   very keen. I had to show them the sights.   The Menin Road thrilled them. They wanted to stand in the middle and pick up stones for souvenirs.   They were excellent fellows, but I expect they thought we lacked enthusiasm.   I did for one.

I was now getting to the end of my tether.   I needed a rest badly.

One night, about 8 p.m., the comparative quiet was broken by very heavy shell fire.   We all repaired to the top of Clapham Junction to see what was happening.   It was worth it.   About five miles away, near Langemarck, a raid or something of the sort was taking place.   Each side was sending up a fine display of coloured rockets, artillery from both sides was firing hard ;

their flashes made the night sparkle. We could see the flames of the shells as they fell and hear the crump of the explosions. Gradually the panic, or whatever it was, spread. The whole salient woke up. More rockets, nearer now. Artillerymen left their dugouts wondering what it was all about. Artillery officers in observation posts thought they had better order a few rounds to be put over. Machine gun crews in the line on both sides fired a belt across No Man's Land just in case. Wires were busy now to various headquarters, enquiries were made, men were hustled from dugouts to man trenches ; in fact, the whole of the salient, always nervous, was now thoroughly awake. The mania reached our front. Behind us a battery fired salvo after salvo. The German batteries replied. We retired to safety and to find out what it was all about.

A raid had been carried out by our troops to the right of Langemarck ; one prisoner taken. · In half an hour all was quiet again.

Soon we were to be relieved. A luncheon party was arranged to welcome the incoming General and his staff. We sat down a party of eight.

Lunch had only just got going when the thud-thud of exploding shells could be heard outside. Syrens shrieked " gas alarm." A shell made a direct hit on our kitchen chimney, with disastrous results. A cloud of gas entered our mess, causing consternation. None of us had gas masks with us. I received the full force of the gas near the door ; luckily it was not very strong. Panic reigned ; my carefully thought-out lunch was forgotten. We were all made to lie down for three hours. The gas was phosgene ; it has a delayed action on the heart, we were told. No ill effects were noticed, however.

We were relieved and I was ordered to report to No. 2 General Hospital, Boulogne, where I remained until my tickets for the south of France arrived.

The first-class return tickets to Mentone were paid for by the members of the Baltic Exchange in London. Our instructions were to proceed to Paris via Amiens, where conveyances would meet us at the Gare du Nord, to take us across to the Gare d' L'Ouest. We arrived in Paris to find motor cars waiting for us, and an excellent dinner prepared at the station. Sleeping berths were reserved for each of us as far as Mentone. There is little to be told about the journey except that it was wonderful to wake up in the morning to find warmth and sunshine instead of the rain and wet of the line.

We arrived at Mentone late the next afternoon, and drove to the Cap Martin Hotel, which had been hired by Lady Michelham. It was in charge of a Colonel. The hotel was run exactly the same as it was in peace time, *i.e.*, we had the same food as the guests would have had, and our bedrooms were simply superb.

I was allotted a room facing the bay of Mentone, on the first floor, the height of comfort, and the dinner that evening was better than one could get at the Carlton Hotel in London at that time. The charge for a cocktail was the enormous sum of one franc. We could have any wine we liked entirely free of charge, with the exception of champagne, for which they charged ten francs a bottle. There was only one rule in the hotel, and, as the Colonel explained, it was not a very arduous one—we were expected to dine in the hotel each night at 7 p.m. For the rest of the day we were entirely our own masters.

Everything had been thought out for our comfort and entertainment. We found the next morning about ten superb motor cars outside the door, which were at our disposal to go for expeditions in the surrounding country at a very low charge. For these expeditions the hotel people supplied excellent luncheon baskets.

The first thing we wanted to do was to go into Monte Carlo, but I am afraid this turned out to be very disappointing, as there were very few people staying there. We were not allowed to go into the Casino in uniform. However, we sampled all the various hotels for lunch and tea all along the Riviera.

On other days we played tennis at the Club. There we met many very charming English girls who were down from the front resting. These girls were on leave from the Women's Ambulance Corps. We soon made it our business to get to know them. There was no difficulty in persuading them to come out to lunch or dinner. They jumped at the chance of a meal at our hotel as there was an abundance of white bread and butter, cream and other luxuries. Also it was very pleasant for two or three of us to ask ladies to dinner when we had not got to pay for it.

One day six of us thought it would be a great plan to take six of these girls over to Nice and stand them a really magnificent lunch at the Hotel Ruhl. We started off in two motor cars, and found that my orders to the manager had been carried out literally, and that he had allotted us a large round table in the famous bow window. The table was decorated entirely with malmaison carnations. I was beginning to wonder what this lunch was going to cost, so I went to interview the maitre d'hotel myself to find he was an old friend of mine from the Piccadilly Hotel. I therefore told him I was somewhat frightened about the carnations, and also about the price of the lunch we had ordered, and he told me that of course the charge would be entirely different as he knew me.

I cannot tell you what we had for lunch, but we all agreed that it was quite the most wonderful meal we had ever eaten. In due course the ladies retired to give us time to settle the bill. We nearly expired when we saw this ; it came to no less than £40. We only just managed to scrape this up amongst the six of us, and we had to borrow money for tips from some of the girls. In consequence the rest of the afternoon was somewhat ruined, as we had no money for tea.

Another day I remember we went to the Hotel Reserve at Beaulieu, as we had heard that they supplied the most wonderful hors d'œuvre. I certainly agreed that they lived up to their reputation. By the time we had finished the hors d'œuvre we had no appetite for anything else.

The time passed very quickly, and about the 18th March I was told I was fit enough to go back to the line, so I left, with great regret, arriving at Amiens on March 20th, where I went to the local headquarters to find out where my brigade was situated.

They told me that they were at a place called Ham, so I got on the 'phone ; the General himself answered, and I was very much mystified by his conversation. He said that above all things I was not to go there ; that he would send my servant with my kit to Amiens for me, as I was due for a month's leave in England. I was delighted to hear this news. However, I felt it would be very ungrateful if I did not go to see them and thank the General personally for all he had done for me, and tell him a little about my trip to the south of France. His reply to this was, " I always knew you were a fool, but now I think you are a much bigger one. However, if you care to come, we shall be pleased to see you."

I arrived at Ham about 8 o'clock on the night of the 20th March, 1918, and found my way to brigade headquarters, which was in a state of feverish activity.

At dinner that night in mess the General and Sanderson told me that the Germans were going to make their big push on a wide front the next day. They told me that the whole of the 5th Army front was very thinly held, but that everything was in readiness for the attack, which they knew was to be launched on the 21st ; the 20th division was to be in corps reserve.

The General said that as I had been absent for such a long time, and as my leave voucher had come through, I had better not cancel my leave under the circumstances. He also told me that General Gough had given instructions that officers proceeding on a month's leave were on no account to be stopped, so I packed my kit ready for the morning, sleeping on the floor in Sanderson's room.

At 5 o'clock in the morning we were awakened by shells dropping in the village, which was surprising, as we were no less than ten miles behind the line, also the roar of gun fire from the front was terrific. On looking out of the window we found that the fog was very thick indeed. We could hardly see across the street.

After a hasty breakfast I said good-bye to them all, and with only a small case walked down the road to the station, where I found the leave party waiting for the train to start. High velocity shells were by this time dropping all around the station. The engine driver was getting more and more nervous ; punctually at 7 a.m. we proceeded on our journey to Boulogne.

We reached the port at about 1 o'clock and proceeded to

report to the landing officer. He was uncertain what to do with us, as all kinds of rumours were flying about that the Germans had broken through. He did not know whether we ought to leave or not.

However, my pass was stamped and I went on board the leave boat. Soon we sailed, even though the fog was very thick.

Two boats at this time started together, escorted by destroyers. All went well until we got three-quarters of the way across, when somewhere out in the fog, not very far from us, there was a deafening explosion. Both the boats immediately stopped ; the destroyers proceeded to go round and round as hard as they could go dropping depth charges. We naturally thought we were being attacked by a German submarine. It was most alarming.

However, in about three-quarters of an hour we proceeded slowly onwards, and eventually landed safely at Folkestone.

CHAPTER XVIII.

ARMISTICE.

LONDON again, with a month's leave.

Somehow I did not feel the same enthusiasm as I had done before. For one thing I slept badly. I could not get to sleep until three and four in the morning. In the day-time I preferred to stay in the hotel and read. Sometimes I had fits of acute depression, imagined that my business affairs were in chaos. I began to think the war would never end ; I was perfectly sure that if I returned to France I would be killed. It became an obsession.

My wife was worried. She took me to see the most prominent nerve specialist of the day. He examined me ; I passed none of his tests, so he sent me away telling me he would write to the Medical Board which was sitting in London.

I didn't care what happened.

When I appeared before the six solemn men a few days later they asked me what was the matter with me. I was questioned by the senior medical officer ; he was very kind. One of the junior members of the board asked me rather aggressively if there was any reason why I should not return to France at the expiration of my leave. I replied that there was no reason why I should not return, and that I was quite prepared to go back if they considered I was in a fit state.

I retired while the board considered my case. The result was that I was granted three months' leave. I was ordered to go to Scotland to fish.

After three peaceful months I once more appeared before the same Board. I told them I was perfectly well. They ordered me to report to headquarters Western Command, Chester, for home service.

I was appointed lecturer to home service units in the Western command on the battles of Langemarck and Cambrai. I can remember most vividly a lecture I gave to about two hundred officers in the Town Hall at Manchester, behind locked doors. Their interest in my account of the Battle of Cambrai was intense. The notes for these lectures have been of the greatest help to me in writing this book.

I returned to London on November 10th, 1918.

At 10-30 a.m., the 11th November, Piccadilly Circus was packed ; very different from the night of August 4th, 1914. A suppressed emotional storm held the crowds ; they were waiting for 11 a.m.

Once again the newsboys rushed into the Circus.

" Armistice signed ! " they shouted.

The storm broke. The crowd went stark, staring mad, the police were powerless. Traffic was held up, taxis and buses were stormed by cheering, yelling men and women ; all social standing went overboard. Men in top hats shook dustmen by the hand, girls kissed perfectly respectable gentlemen they had never seen before. Total strangers walked arm-in-arm to places of refreshment to celebrate the news ; the air was full of streamers ; the noise of syrens, motor horns, rattles and whistles was deafening.

I was propelled towards Buckingham Palace. The colossal crowd cheered themselves hoarse when His Majesty appeared.

The doings in London that night were indescribable. I can vaguely remember dining with a crowd of friends at some restaurant. I don't remember anything more.

The war was over.

CHAPTER XIX.

CONCLUSION.

THE Great War is now history.

The rising generation never give it a thought except when they realise that a serious shortage of money is affecting their parents ; and incidentally themselves, when they discover how difficult it is to find employment in any sphere of life.

Surely it is time that they began to take an intelligent and comprehensive interest in the last war, for if there is to be another, it is they who will have to do the fighting.

If the prophets are to be believed, the young generation may take part in another war VERY SOON.

When they can find time to read a book like this one, let them try to imagine their feelings on hearing the scream of a 5.9 shell coming uncomfortably close ; or waking up at night to the ominous drone of hostile planes immediately over their heads.

Most of the combatants in the Great War lived in a continuous state of fear when in the fighting area. We had to try and accustom ourselves to being afraid. We could not allow our minds to dwell upon the loss of those very near to us, nor upon the fact that our friends of to-day might be killed or terribly maimed to-morrow. Nor did we allow our imaginations to wonder how long we, ourselves, would survive. Such thoughts would have spelt disaster and possible disgrace. It became obligatory to hide all inner thoughts and feelings, and to be apparently callous to horrible sights.

As that ghastly contest dragged on month after month, and year after year, many of us felt our will power and our nerve weakening. Depression came with a sense of despair. Would the war never come to an end ?

Those of us who have got through and are still alive can never forget the experience. Many of us have got sons who may have to take the part that their fathers took in the last war. They will have to fight for their country, and most of them will have to fight as infantry.

It is obvious that the Great War was a picnic in comparison with what the next war will be.

Our sons will have to endure far worse terrors than their fathers did, who were only called upon to fight against a foe armed with rifles, bombs and bayonets, supported by machine guns and massed artillery. Offensive weapons have been improved out of all knowledge since the Armistice.

It is a grim prospect for the infantry in the next war.

They will have to face concerted attacks from incredibly fast, low-flying planes and high speed tanks. Fourteen years ago the design of these machines was almost in its infancy. The Allied troops were never called upon to resist tanks, although the Germans must realise fully the terror that these newly-invented instruments of war infused into their half-beaten armies.

To-day all the armies of the world, with the exception of Germany, are equipped with highly efficient tanks.

The infantry of the future will, of course, be armed with the latest anti-tank and anti-aircraft devices. Tactics have been changed in order to meet the increased speed and potency of attack in modern warfare ; but there is a limit to the courage of the finest infantry in the world . . . the limit of human endurance.

It seems doubtful if the weapons provided for defence will give the infantry sufficient confidence to hold on to their positions when assailed by hordes of tanks and low-flying planes. Is it not probable that modern weapons of war have now reached such a pitch of mechanisation that the human soldier will not be able to stand against them ?

Will infantry be useless ?

At the present moment the General Staffs of all nations still consider that infantry are the backbone of their armies for defensive and offensive operations.

If, in another war, infantry proved a failure, it might mean that neither side could force a decision, in which case the struggle might continue until our present civilisation would be almost annihilated.

Another world war would be a disaster of such magnitude that no one living can foretell the results. Yet, to-day, every nation is spending millions of pounds on armaments, because they dare not be found unprepared.

The existing apathy of the people of the world in general shown towards the possibility of another war is incomprehensible.   Somehow they must be made to understand its perils, that is, if civilisation is to continue as we know it to-day.

Those of us who fought in the last war realise that another war, magnified to hideous proportions, would mean utter disaster to the nations concerned.

It is, therefore, the duty of every citizen, young or old, of all nationalities, to encourage those who are working for the settlement of international disputes by peaceful means ; to remove the causes of war, and to ostracize the aggressor from the Community of Nations.

THE END.